I0223446

Cat Tracks

A Budget Train Travel Adventure

Insights And Images
From California To New England

By Cat Cohen

Published by Cat Cohen Unltd
Road Horizons Division

OTHER BOOKS by CAT COHEN

Road Horizon Division
MY DESERT BLOG CABIN (2009/2013)
A real estate memoir of how the author came to build his home in a rural settlement twenty miles north of Palm Springs.

TALES OF A CENSUS WORKER (2011)
A journal of the author's experiences while canvassing small town citizens, horse ranchers, fearful Hispanics, and anti-government holdouts for the 2010 census in the Southern California high desert.

ROAD STORIES SOUTHWEST (2010/2013)
Way-Off-the-beaten-path travel adventures from three journeys in New Mexico, Arizona, Southern Colorado and Northeastern Baja California.

ROAD POEMS U.S.A. [Snapshots in Verse] (2010)
Insightful observations and photos from the author's coast-to-coast journeys from southwest to northeast and points in between.

THE LONGER ROAD HOME (2015)
An inspiring novel of recovery narrated by Sam Freberg, a bohemian Jewish musician born into a dysfunctional LA family in the 1940s,-his struggle for self-acceptance as a gay man, and how he combats addictions and an AIDS diagnosis.

Savory Publications Division
CHICKEN SOUPS FROM AROUND THE WORLD (2011)
Chicken soup recipes from 39 countries covering techniques and ingredients from equatorial Africa to arctic Alaska and very many temperate zones.

WHINE CONNOISSEUR'S GUIDE (2009/2013)
co-author Avry Budka   A tongue-in-cheek guide to the history of whines, whinemaker's art, whining and dining, whines for every occasion.

DIVING OUT IN LA (1984/1986)
co-author Avry Budka   A nostalgic and witty cult classic guide to the best low-cost eateries in the Greater Los Angeles area during the 1980s.

Koan Music Division
WRITING AND MARKETING SONGS FOR AN ORIGINAL ACT (2013)
An informative discussion of important songwriting issues questions such as performance, message, audience, genre, style, and industry format.

CAT TRACKS
A BUDGET TRAIN TRAVEL ADVENTURE

Written by Cat Cohen
Edited by Avry Budka
Photographs by Cat Cohen
Additional photographs courtesy of Dreamstime

ISBN # 978-0-9899390-5-8

Library of Congress Control Number 2018903092
Published by Cat Cohen Unltd

Printed in the United States of America

Cat Cohen Unltd
ROAD HORIZONS DIVISION
PO Box 275   Morongo Valley, CA 92256

cat@catcohen.com   www.catcohenauthor.com

First Edition – March, 2018

Aloof and light-hearted I take to the open road
Healthy, free, the world before me,
The long brown path before me leading me wherever I choose

Henceforth I ask not good-fortune, I myself am good-fortune
Henceforth I whimper no more, postpone no more, need nothing
Done with indoor complaints, libraries, querulous criticisms,
Strong and content I travel the open road

Walt Whitman

ACKNOWLEDGEMENTS

I want to express my appreciation to Avry Budka, my self-titled editrix, for ironing out countless kinks in this text and guiding me though the challenges of staying true to my experiences while keeping the descriptions engaging and entertaining.

I also want to thank my friends Rush Rushton and Ronni Solman who not only let me stay at their summer beach house in Gloucester, MA, but also showed me around the area as only local residents are able to do.

In addition, I am grateful to my cousin Louise Koroluk and her husband Igor who graciously hosted me in their home outside of Albany, NY and another cousin Deborah Beck-Olson and her husband Bill who did the same at their residence in Peekskill, NY.

What helped to make my travels so rewarding were the many wonderful fellow travelers who shared train and plane seats, guests who conversed with me at hostel sofas and tables, and caring professionals in the hospitality industry who assisted me throughout my itinerary.

Finally, while getting this work ready for publication, I received helpful ideas and support from several fellow members of the Palm Springs Writers Guild and I want to extend my gratitude to them.

Disclaimer

CAT TRACKS – A Budget Train Travel Adventure is based on the author's journal of a cross-country trip undertaken in September 2012. Though the people and places are real, the author has attempted to avoid specific names that could possibly cause anyone discomfort.

Two roads converged in a wood, and I,
I took the road less traveled by
And that has made all the difference

Robert Frost

FOREWORD

This book is proof that cross-country travel does not need to be complicated, stressful, or expensive. By doing a fair amount of research beforehand, I was able to scope out interesting and reasonably priced places at which to dine and stay for the night. Through a successful combination of pre-planning and freewheeling I had a wonderful 15 days of adventure and a cornucopia of meaningful experiences. If this journal motivates anyone else to undertake a similar journey, I would be very pleased.

Love and enlightenment to all,

Cat Cohen

On journeys through the States we start,
Ay through the world, urged by these songs
Sailing henceforth to every land, to every sea
We willing learners of all, teachers of all, lovers of all

Walt Whitman

TABLE OF CONTENTS

INTRODUCTION

2012 started out as a challenging year. Having just become a senior citizen, I was adjusting to the mixed emotions of entering a new chapter in my life. Though grateful to have reached this milestone intact, I was wasn't especially thrilled about encountering a few challenges that came along with aging such as decreasing mobility and increasing physical discomfort. Confronting this situation motivated me to utter the term ''bucket list' under my breath more than a few times.

As my ability to withstand strenuous travel activity was diminishing, my lifelong appetite for travel and adventure was not. At the same time, pursuing and scouting new experiences on the road seemed to be odds with my modest Social Security and self-employment income. This necessitated formulating the ability to travel as fully and freely as I could on a limited budget. No stranger to traveling on the cheap, having done this throughout much of my life, especially in my college and young adult years, I took on the challenge with gusto.

Eschewing professional travel agents including the ones at my local AAA chapter, I steeped myself in travel guides and other sourcebooks at my public library. Going online, I consulted countless internet sites. There I found a treasure trove of tips and recommendations for inexpensive modes of transportation, value-oriented accommodations, and reasonably priced eateries. Especially helpful was a guide to youth hostels across America. Knowing that website listings like Yelp and Trip Advisor can't always be taken at face value, I searched for the buzzwords that seemed to reflect my particular taste and values. Many of these descriptions turned out well while others led me to places I didn't feel were worth experiencing. Even when a listing appeared to be disappointing, pursuing them enabled me to see sights and neighborhoods in cities and towns I might not have visited.

Armed with all this information, I had a primitive grid of the main streets and attractions of each place on my route beforehand. This made it easier to make decisions and choose paths in one unfamiliar setting after another. Balancing prior research and ad hoc improvisation, I was able to craft a train, rent-a-car, and cheap flight itinerary that gave me a lot of bang for my buck. I managed to keep my 15-day trek to under $75 a day for all expenses paid. Staying within this price range, I managed to have both a memorable and wonderful time.

MORONGO BASIN TO NEW MEXICO
SUNDAY - SEPTEMBER 9

The month of September is one of my favorite times of year to travel. This is after summer crowds have thinned and there still is abundant sunlight and comfortable weather. I planned a mixture of train and rented car transportation, mostly riding the rails from Southern California to the Atlantic coast, then jetting back. Unlike prior cross-country trips that started in LA, because of a recent move to just north of the Palm Springs area, I began this journey in my new high desert environs.

I asked a friend to drive me from my Morongo Basin home to the train station at Victorville. We started off crossing the Mojave Desert on a lonely stretch of 2-lane highway 247 that passes the hamlets of Flamingo Heights, Landers, Johnson Valley, and Lucerne Valley. Little did I know what great contrasts in scenery and life styles awaited me. Joshua trees, spindly yucca plants, large boulders, and dry lakes would soon be replaced by a plethora of new images. In the past, I'd been a traveler from a metropolitan center. This time I was an ex-urb, a small town resident with a whole new point of view.

Turning onto Route 18 at Apple Valley, we arrived as twilight fell at the Victorville station. I expected a large building with well-lit benches and infrastructure. Instead, there was only a bus stop bench under a dimly lit plastic overhang. At nine pm, along with three other travelers I boarded the Amtrak **Southwest Chief** headed east to Chicago.

The coach car was half empty. Not only did I have my choice of where to sit, there were double seats available to sleep in. Once I got settled, there wasn't anything to see outside on this new moon dark night. So I said sayonara to the day and looked forward to waking up on the road, most likely somewhere in Arizona. The rolling motion of the train rocked me to sleep like a mother singing a lullaby.

My heart is warm with the friends I make
Add better friends I'll not be knowing
Yet there isn't a train I wouldn't take
No matter where it's going

Edna St Vincent Millay

The author's backyard in the Morongo Basin

The author walking his dog Stella along joshua trees a few miles from his home

NEW MEXICO TO KANSAS CITY
MONDAY - SEPTEMBER 10

Forgetting that I'd set my wristwatch alarm to 7am, I was roused from much needed slumber by surprise. I gazed out the window expecting to be near Winslow, Arizona. Instead, I saw a highway sign with the words Welcome To New Mexico in large letters. Simultaneously, a voice came over the loudspeaker announcing that we were crossing over the state border and needed to set our watches an hour ahead to Mountain Daylight Time.

Paralleling the train tracks was an arid region of red earth gullies and dusty gray-green shrubbery and pinyon pines. A rainstorm had fallen the night before. The normally dry creeks had rivulets of water. Chugging its way through this exotic landscape, the train approached the Indian town of Gallup. Picturesque vistas like this are never seen when crossing the U.S. by plane. I was glad to be on board.

Feeling groggy, every cell in my body cried out for coffee. This necessitated a walk to the scenicruiser lounge two cars away where the snack bar was located. As the train swung from side-to-side, I did a balancing act through the coach and down a flight of stairs where I ordered some fresh java. On the way back, a hyperactive three-year old girl was using the stairway as her own private playground, screaming gleefully as she raced up and down. Part of me wanted to yell at her to get out of my way so I could satisfy my java jones. But captivated by her playfulness, I played dodgeball, matching her jumps and giggles as I ascended to the observation area.

I gratified my caffeinated cravings while gazing at the sights of the New Mexico countryside whizzing by. A cup of yoghurt completed my simple breakfast. I was saving my appetite for a scheduled hour's service stop at Albuquerque around noon where I planned to put on my track shoes and seek out a bowl of green chili, the state's signature dish, for lunch.

After running up and down the steps of the lounge car, the little girl finally sat next her mother at the table across from me. I breathed a sigh of relief. This respite from toddler activity was short-lived. She ran over to join me at my table and proudly stated that her name was Zoe. Then she shouted to her mom that I was her new friend. I wrote 'Z-O-E" down in large letters so she could see it, and she liked this. I asked if she could tell me

Observation lounge car

the colors of the flowers in the fields we were passing. Each one of the many-colored blooms that I pointed out she said were yellow. I then asked her to name the colors of the homes on the sides of the tracks. Once again, they all were yellow. Evidently, she hadn't yet learned the names of the other colors. If I had any crayons with me, I would have given her a box.

Zoe went back to her mother and announced that I was now her new best friend. What a big promotion for so little work. Her mom smiled at me, obviously approving of our being pals. When I remarked how lucky she was to have such an outgoing child, she nodded knowingly. They left the lounge car to return to their seats, and I did the same.

On the way back, I made an exploratory tour of the train, such as it was at the time — two coach cars, the lounge car, and the dining car. Several sleeper cars in the front were restricted to the people who'd reserved them. I heard from the snack bar server that more coaches and sleepers would be added at our stop in Albuquerque.

At my seat, I imagined that Zoe was probably playing with her toys. So I started playing with one of mine, an Android smart phone I'd recently purchased. I got out the instruction manual and studied how to navigate it. Besides making phone calls, I now had the ability to take pictures of my trip and log on to the internet for searches and information. This little hand-held device had more power and storage space than my entire desktop computer at home. There was a big learning curve, so I kept consulting my manual, enduring a lot of trial and error. Just when I was congratulating myself for getting the hang of it, I looked around to see many passengers working their phones as well. If I thought I was getting a leg up on the crowd, it seemed I was only keeping pace with them.

When we reached Gallup, outside my window were many motels with colorful signs. This travel center has as many independent motels as franchises, a holdover from its Route 66 days. When we arrived at the station, a portly gentleman dramatically opened a large iron gate for travelers entering or departing. It looked like a movie setting, a lama opening temple gates in Tibet. On my new toy I snapped a few photos, then turned my attention to the array of Indian curio stores.

One shop caught my eye, a Zuni Fetish Store. I had no idea if their merchandise was for spiritual ceremonies or something more sinister, a Native American equivalent of DeSade. Undoubtedly, the former. This colorful city isn't known as an adult movie center. I would have taken a stroll outside, but our stop here was short and we were soon on our way.

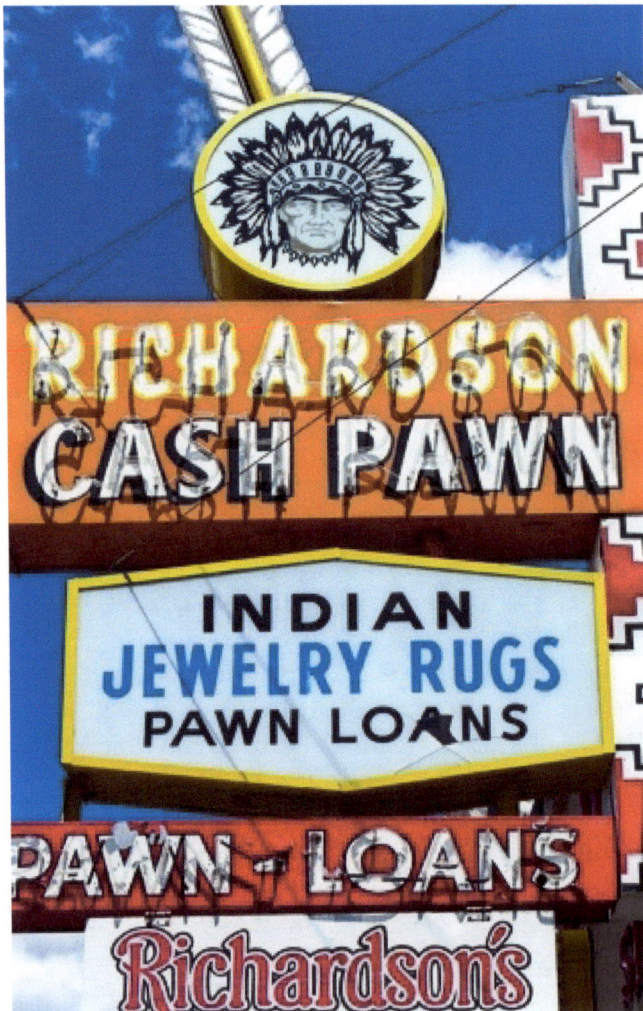

Curio Store, Gallup, NM

A little east of Gallup, the tracks followed the path of Route 66, its original buildings exhibiting cultural kitsch. Over the years, I learned to weed out the over-the-top turista elements to find some authentic merchandise there. Despite all its cheesiness, this roadway is a fun slice of Americana.

Route 66 Diner, East of Gallup, NM

At Albuquerque, we arrived at our service break thirty minutes early. I now had an hour and a half to depart and explore. Though encouraged to get off the train, we were all warned to be back on time. When pulling out of the station, Amtrak waits for no one.

I was salivating for a bowl of green chili at a Southwest style cafe, but all I could find nearby were franchised international eateries that served food like Italian, Chinese, or Japanese. After walking several blocks searching for a regional restaurant without success, I noticed a pub with an intriguing menu. Besides featuring several microbrewery beers, the signature dish I was hankering for was offered.

I sat down at a table on the sidewalk in front and treated myself to some homemade stew with large chunks of pork in a savory green chili and tomatillo sauce with all the fixings. The trendy twenty-something waitress was friendly and efficient, and the food was as prepared as well as any I've had in New Mexico.

After a leisurely paced meal, I took a walking tour. Though not in the best of neighborhoods, the main thoroughfare was undergoing gentrification and there were many fashionable boutiques and trendy art galleries among the dilapidated liquor stores and pawnshops. On the way back to the train, I passed a district of historic churches with rounded domes, graceful Spanish arches and many other unique ornate architectural details. I very much enjoyed this unique juxtaposition of old and new.

Brew Pub, Albuquerque, NM

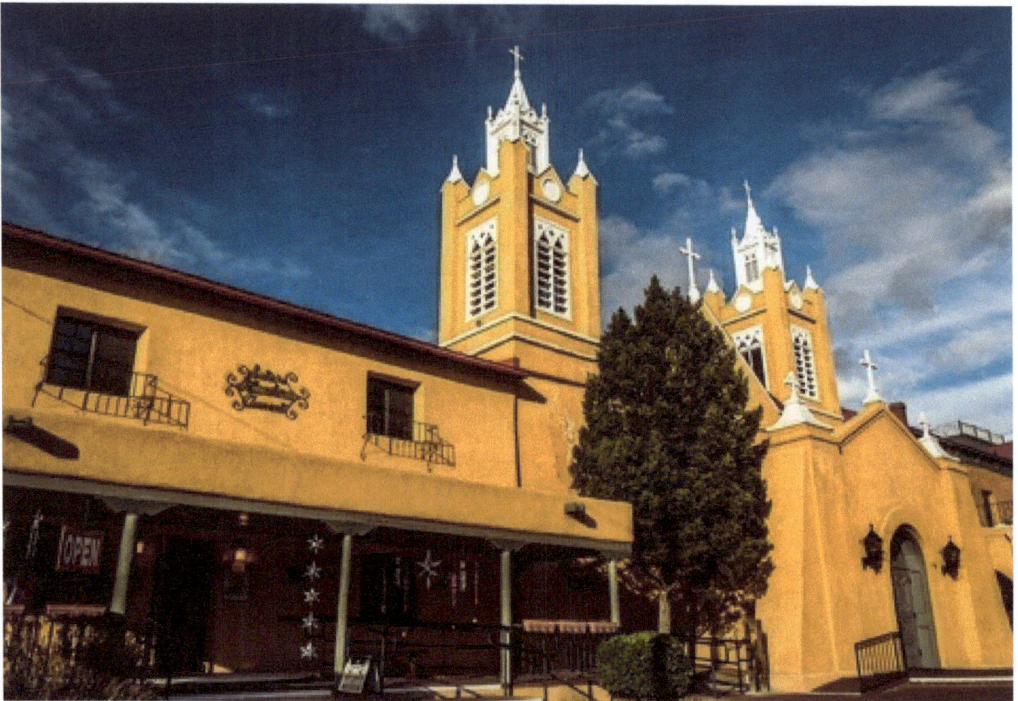

Shops And Church, Albuquerque, NM

The train I boarded was twice as long as the one I left 90 minutes earlier. Our next stop was Las Vegas, not the Nevada casino capital, but one of the oldest settlements in the state. Only departing passengers were allowed to leave the train, so I had to limit my observation to what I could see through the windows.

There was an old hotel located next to the tracks. One had a close-up view of this once sought-after elegant house of hospitality and its well-landscaped grounds. A loudspeaker voice informed us that this grand structure was a place where Teddy Roosevelt met regularly with his Rough Rider buddies. The building had a brick foundation decorated with detailed bas-relief that harkened back to a day when workmanship and craft were executed at a very high level. I could see a large presidential entourage here in its heyday.

Unlike the movie, the train began "Leaving Las Vegas" with neither Nicholas Cage nor Sheryl Crow on board. We soon passed a patchwork quilt of dusty green pine clusters that alternated with sparse dry grassland. No overcrowded planet existed here. Not a solitary person, building, or roadway was anywhere to be seen.

In a half hour, we entered a dark tunnel in Raton Pass and came out on the Colorado side. All greenery was left behind. Above a vista of unrelenting flatness, jagged Pikes Peak atop the Rocky Mountains loomed in the distance to the west. This was awesome, but so stark I'd never want to be stranded in this remote countryside.

Scattered herds of cattle, if you can call a dozen animals grazing on meager grass a herd, seemed like slim pickings in these vast pastures. I've read about cowboys escorting cattle through this region to and from Texas. As long as it was in the warmer months, this was doable.

The winters here must be severe and hostile. I could almost hear the cowhands singing in the hinterland "Get along little doggies, get me to San Antone before the weather turns nasty" as they marched their charges to market on the old Santa Fe Trail.

A few tiny settlement towns were the only ones we passed in this forlorn area. Trinidad, an unlikely candidate for notoriety in this conservative part of the country has become infamous as the "Sex Change Capital of the U.S.," primarily because one of its medical practitioners, Stanley Biber, specialized in sexual reassignment surgery. For a while, the phrase "taking a trip to Trinidad" was a euphemism for changing one's gender.

Since the train didn't stop here, there were no transgender arrivals or departures. Imagine coming in as Roy Rogers and leaving as Dale Evans. In this one-horse town, what would Trigger think, let alone Mr. Ed? Not unless he had a closet desire to be Mrs. Ed.

About fifty miles further east was the town of La Junta. Its main claim to fame is that it used to be a stop on the Atchison, Topeka, and Santa Fe Railroad. This former trading post is the home of a museum with a collection of Native American artifacts and is the site of a Boy Scout program that trains young men in Indian dance and costumes.

This small town has an authentic Mayberry feel. The central district of long established small shops and businesses took my imagination to bygone days. Without even a train station here for folks to come and go, this isolated place was truly a time warp.

House near the tracks just outside of La Junta, CO

We then travelled through a long stretch without any towns or settlements. Tired of the monotonous landscape, I took refuge in the lounge car. As daylight faded, I struck up a conversation with a fellow from Cleveland. We talked about his hometown. I asked him if, like most cities in the Rust Belt, it had lost much population. He replied affirmatively, but since the opening of some new museums, especially the Rock 'n Roll Hall Of Fame, this trend is reversing. Young people have moved into the downtown warehouses, restoring the area with arty shops, chic restaurants, and live theaters. He said Cleveland has one of the largest theater districts in the U.S. It's funny how we from LA and New York think that we are the only ones with artistic life.

By the time the train crossed from Colorado into Kansas, darkness fell. An announcement told us to move our watches ahead another hour for Central Daylight time. Until that moment, it had never dawned on me that that these two widely differing states, one famous for its jagged Rocky Mountains and the other known for its Great Plains and wheat fields, are contiguous. This part of the U.S. may seldom get any notice, but its gritty character of seemingly endless flat earth and big sky is a welcome respite from contemporary urban life.

When another announcement blurted that it was last call for the dining car, I hurried there for dinner. I was seated with three other passengers at a table set with an elegant cloth, a vase of fresh flowers, and linen napkins, a throwback to the traditional hospitality of yesteryear. Having seen many films with similar formal place settings, it was a pleasure to experience this first hand. I hadn't experienced dining on fine china and sipping beverages in expensive glassware in a while.

While vestiges of twilight faded outside, we each placed orders with our waiter. As we introduced ourselves, I discovered that we hailed from widely different locales. The middle-aged man next to me was a photo instructor from Maryland, a woman in her sixties sitting across from me was a recently retired rail worker from Kansas, a third diner was a retired housewife from a coastal town near Santa Barbara, and yours truly was the lone high desert rat. The meals brought to our table were worthy of any fine dining establishment, artfully served by the friendly Amtrak staff.

In this lively group, a recurrent topic was the challenging new internet technology and why we all needed to curry relationships with twelve-year-olds who were much more familiar than us with the changing world of electronic gear. This was followed by nostalgic memories of how simple life had been before these new apparatuses arrived, how complicated and isolating the world was becoming because of the cyber revolution we were living through.

I'd already observed that most of the young people on the train were so busy with their gadgets that they hardly looked to see where we were traveling. We oldsters appeared to be the only ones enjoying our cross-country trip, not needing to distract ourselves for the duration. Seasoned Amtrak riders like us appreciate the leisurely pace of train travel and its opportunities for sightseeing and social interaction. The fact most of us were retired or only working part-time probably added to this discrepancy.

I left my delightful dinner companions feeling like I'd dined with friends. With little to see or do on the train in the evening, and tired of logging on to my smart-phone, I called it a day. Back in my coach seat, I fell asleep to the undulations of the train's movements.

Night from a railroad car window
Is a great, dark, soft thing
Broken across with slashes of light

Carl Sandburg

KANSAS CITY TO CHICAGO
TUESDAY - SEPTEMBER 11

On this infamous anniversary, I didn't mind being away from the day's commemoration of one of the most alarming events in American history. Immersing myself in an extended media onslaught of all that unfortunate loss of life and destruction of property was not how I wanted to spend my vacation. I'd planned to wake at dawn to view scenes of Kansas outside, but I slept too late to see any sights. Instead, I was awakened when the train stopped suddenly on a sidetrack outside of Kansas City, Missouri. We had to wait until a freight train with well over a hundred cars passed before we could continue.

Union Station and Downtown Skyline, Kansas City, MO

Instead of a long service break, our stay here was relatively short. I'd hoped to walk the streets downtown where I could view some of this Midwestern metropolis's famed architecture, but the entrance to the train station faced the opposite direction, denying convenient access. With no way for my feet to explore the area, I was forced to observe what I could from the platform.

Once we were back in motion, we were soon in the countryside with its large sprawling farms. Before long, the last call for breakfast was announced. I made a hasty effort to meet this deadline. Rushing past the additional cars added during our stop, I barely made it in time.

The dining car was divided into two parts, one near the coach seats and the other adjacent to the sleeper cars. I was seated at a table on the sleeper (patrician) side along with two nondescript Southern California suburbanites, a far cry from the colorful group I'd dined with the night before. Sleeper customers have all meals included with their tickets. I noticed that I was the only one in this section with a tab, the lone coach diner. I didn't know if it was class distinction or simply the luck of the draw, but my companions and I had little in common. Conversation between us was minimal, cordial at best.

The only interesting aspect of the meal was the Amish-looking family sitting at the table across from us. Dressed in clothing out of the nineteenth century, they were formal and restrained. As backward as this young family of four appeared to be, I wondered how they could afford the luxury of their sleeping car surroundings. In their odd dress and polite demeanor, they interested me far more than the middle-aged men wearing golf shirts seated at my table.

I tried to engage them in conversation. When I inquired, the man answered while the other family members remained stone-faced. I learned that they were from Colorado, not Pennsylvania as I had assumed. They were Mennonites, not Amish. When I asked what he did for a living, the man signaled he did not want to talk further. I wished the family well and had to imagine their austere life style from afar.

The landscape we passed through next was as dry as my breakfast conversations. We passed a severely drought-stricken area, one that had been reported on the news. It was sad to see fields of ruined crops and yellowed grassland. 2012 had been the driest summer in over 50 years, and this part of Missouri was paying a heavy price for Mother Nature's neglect. Cornfields were either left unattended or dug under. Alfalfa and other crops also sustained damage. I felt sorry for the farmers who'd been forced to count the year as a loss.

I paid my tab and returned to the lounge car where I could get a better view of this distressed countryside.   I sat next to a portly gentleman who was chatting with a slim, feisty, elderly lady. They were sharing farming concerns, especially the effects of climate change, a phenomenon they confessed that they'd only recently begun to be convinced of. This subject being near and dear to my heart, I became a fly on the wall and listened intently.

The man had been a farmer in this area. Having left agriculture a few years earlier, he said that most of his colleagues were having a rough time. The woman was an orchard grower from central Michigan, also with tales of a difficult year. She grew a wide variety of fruit to can and preserve for her roadside produce stand. She complained not of drought, but about the unseasonal weather that brought a warm winter and a very cold spring. This confused her fruit trees. They bloomed out of season, and she lost most of her crop. She added that the sour cherry harvest on the Upper Peninsula had been totally wiped out.

I chimed into their conversation, having experienced something similar in the high desert where my peach, apricot, plum, and cherry trees lost their fruit to late cold spells. Another hardship the ex-farmer talked about was how water management wars were being fought near his town forcing growers to switch to drip irrigation after decades of easy access. He felt these were omens of things to come.

Another topic raised by the Michigan woman was that of her recent experiences with beekeeping, both its joys and pitfalls. She talked about the importance of maintaining an optimum queen-to-worker bee ratio, and how this was also undermined by the unpredictable weather. If the winter was warm enough, the queens lived through it. All she needed to buy was a few new drones. But after months of gyrating temperatures, she had to start over from scratch. This year had brought her poor results. We agreed that the past few months had indeed been challenging for many.

A few more farm recollections were followed by some good barnyard jokes. I bid farewell to my rural travel mates and returned to my seat. After we crossed the Mississippi River into Illinois, I focused on the transition from expansive farm country to increasing urbanization as we made our way to Chicago. Acres of former fields had become sprawling new housing tracts. Constructed in a hybrid of modern and traditional styles, these new communities were set in a verdant area with lovely forested hills and tranquil streams.

What surprised me was the complete absence of fences around these homes. In the West, although our libertarian theme is "don't fence me in," it is almost unheard of to have such open properties. Interspersed every few miles with these pleasant residential neighborhoods, recently built commercial areas featured colorful shops, restaurants, and occasional big box stores.

As we got closer to our destination, the business districts became larger and the houses were older and less affluent. Hardscrabble neighborhoods with graffiti scrawled on the walls and shabby brick houses and dilapidated apartments became the norm. The tracks led through blocks of the kind of ugly industrial waste often found next to rail lines in large metropolitan areas.

It wasn't long before downtown Chicago's majestic skyline appeared in the distance. An intercom announcement advised us to prepare for imminent departure. I collected my gear to get ready for a Chicago adventure that included a late lunch in Greektown, a neighborhood not far from the station.

Union Station, Chicago, IL

Because the train depot was so large, it was an effort to drag my wheeled luggage to the street. The weather was very warm for September. In my travel weary state, I struggled with my bags the few blocks to the Greek community. Fondly remembering an eatery from a few years back, I was looking forward to a great meal. But the café had changed hands. Greek food was no longer served there.

Too tired to undertake a search for an alternative, I went to a Greek cafe across the street. This place was not as pleasant inside, the room not air-conditioned, and the food was nothing special. But I was served a decent ethnic meal at a reasonable price.

Afterwards, I made my way down the block and passed what might have been a better choice. At its appealing bakery, I consoled myself with a few small pastries and a cup of strong coffee.   Buoyed by the sugar rush, I got the wherewithal to continue to my night's destination, a youth hostel that I'd booked online.

My map said that this site was only a few blocks away. Feeling more energetic, instead of boarding a bus, I attempted to walk there.   This was a poor decision. It was rush hour and the sidewalks were filled with people. To make matters worse, the map did not mention that the area between Greektown and the hostel was undergoing street repair. There were so many detours, my five-block walk took more than three times the time and effort I'd expected.

By the time I arrived at the hostel, I was tanked out. Despite this, my spirits were lifted when I found the place situated in one of Chicago's best neighborhoods alongside its most expensive hotels. Nearby was Grant Park with its beautiful grounds and great view of Lake Michigan.

The hostel housed what the guidebooks had correctly described as the Rolls Royce of budget stays. Good-looking fashionable young people from all over the world were gathered in the lobby. The front room was decorated in a contemporary style with very high ceilings and attractive murals on the walls. This place was clean, organized, and inviting, not a step down as hostels can be, but a step up.

Registering at the front desk, I was given a card key to a room on the third floor that I was to occupy with seven other men in a dormitory bunk bed and shared bathroom situation. After sleeping in a very public Amtrak coach seat the previous two nights, it sounded just fine.

Entering the room, I found it as appealing as the downstairs. There were four bunk beds, several lockers, and a private toilet and shower in the bathroom with common sinks outside for washing up and shaving. A shelf by the shower displayed a large variety of shampoos and toiletries for all to use. Not even in a fancy Las Vegas hotel was I given as many choices. There were electric outlets on every wall, a welcome convenience for charging smart phones, laptops and such. An extra bonus was the free breakfast in the morning. At one-fourth the rate of most Chicago hotel rooms, this place was a find.

My roost for the night was the upper bunk on the left. I put a few items on top to claim my territory and stowed my luggage in a locker with the bunk bed number on it. Then I freshened up and walked outside, relieved to be carrying only a few light things in a day pack for a change. In the open spaces of Grant Park, I tried to decompress.

No sooner than I sat down at a park bench than the sound system started playing symphonic arrangements of patriotic songs and Gershwin tunes. I felt like I was at an outdoor concert as I stared at the waters of Lake Michigan and took in the balmy evening air.   What a change from pop music blaring from car radios and leaking from train travelers' headphones. As the sun set over the downtown skyscrapers, the architecture was as grand as anything in Manhattan or LA. The colorful lighting displays of the park's Buckingham Fountain made me glad I'd decided to spend time there.

The warm weather had brought a crowd to the park including a group of twenty-somethings parading on their motorized scooters and several families with young children running around. This place felt amazingly safe for such an urban setting. As night enveloped the sky, I people-watched and savored the pleasant atmosphere. The tall buildings were lit up in such a dramatic fashion, the skyline made an even more impressive statement at night than in the daytime.

Fountain in Grant Park, Chicago, IL

Later, I made my way back to the hostel to find that I was the first one in my room to turn in for the night. I suspected that the young crowd here was enjoying taking advantage of the city's night scene. I probably was the oldest person in this youthful establishment, but that didn't faze me. After a very long and full day, I climbed up the ladder to my waiting repose, got under the covers, and gratefully fell asleep.

The world's an inn, and I her guest
I eat, I drink, I take my rest
My hostess, nature does deny me
Nothing, wherewith she can supply me
Where, having stayed a while, I pay
Her lavish bills, and go my way

Francis Quarles

CHICAGO TO INDIANA
WEDNESDAY - SEPTEMBER 12

In the middle of the night, as nature would have it, I awoke and needed to use the facilities. The room was dark. In the dim light I could see that most of the other bunks were occupied. Groping around, I observed that I needed to climb down the ladder from my roost. In my groggy state this was easier said than done. I was still wearing socks and almost slipped off the ladder twice as I desperately hung onto the side rails. It would have been embarrassing to fall and wake up the others, not to mention injure myself.

After using the private bathroom, I took off my socks before climbing back up. This did not make the ascent any less treacherous. I barely avoided slipping off the ladder again, grabbing onto the handholds in a panic. I could just hear my young roommates disparaging having an old fuddy-duddy ruining their sleep, needing to administer first aid in the middle of the night.

Thanking my lucky stars after successfully completing this hazardous maneuver, I had just safely crawled under my covers when the room started reverberating with a loud noise. The young man in the bunk below me was snoring, and his impaired breathing was very irritating. I hoped I'd just woken him up into a half-sleep and that he'd soon saw off a few logs and get past this. My wish for quiet was not granted. He continued these rumblings, every now and then stopping breathing for short periods, then resuming his aural static.

I'd traveled cross-country in a train car with over sixty people and not a snorer was heard in the whole bunch. Now in this room of only eight sleepers, try as I might, I could not block him out. I heard other guys in the room tossing and turning in the same manner as me. Knowing I wasn't alone in being disturbed was not comforting. I wanted to make a complaint to the desk clerk, or hit the guy in the face with a pillow. At 3am, neither of these options were doable.

We endured over 30 minutes of this sleep apnial symphony. Finally, the snorer changed his body position. My wide-awake nightmare came to an end. I was so agitated that it took a while to fall asleep again. I prayed that when this occurred I wouldn't wake up and need another bathroom visit.

Fortunately, from that time on my repose was uninterrupted. In the morning, I awoke to a room abuzz with men less than half my age in various stages of showering, shaving, and getting dressed. When I carefully climbed down from my perch, some of them had left. Everyone, including the young snorer, was sensitive and respectful, no rotten apples in this group. I did my best to treat them in kind.

For my morning ritual, I sampled a few of the wide array of toiletry products in the bathroom and readied myself to face the world. There was no need to pack my gear right away. I had plenty of time to go to the main room on the second floor and enjoy a complementary breakfast before needing to check out.

The mess hall reminded me of my college dorm cafeteria. Juice, coffee, cereal, toast, and waffles were laid out in containers. The room sat over a hundred young men and women at tables of four apiece. Most of the diners were in their twenties or thirties. A few middle-aged people were there. I was the lone senior citizen in the room. These places aren't called youth hostels for nothing.

Finding an available spot, I sat myself down at a table with three young men. My breakfast mates were from Uruguay, Mexico, and South Africa. My Spanish speaking ability helped start a conversation with Mr. Uruguay, a young man with limited English skills. He was from Montevideo, the capital, and traveled here to take a short course at a local university. The hostel was close to his campus.

The fellow from Mexico refused to converse in his native language, only speaking English. He was a high-tech entrepreneur with his own start-up calibration company. The main reason for his visit was a trade show in the area that allowed him to promote his business and do some networking.   I asked him if the politics in Mexico helped or hindered his efforts. He got little assistance from the government. Despite this, he had no complaints with any officials.

The South African man, a vendor at the same show, was an ex-pat who considered Memphis, Tennessee to be his new hometown. Of Dutch Boer descent, he had no discernable accent, speaking instead with a thick southern drawl. When I asked how he'd picked this up, he said he wanted to blend in with the contractors he worked with. With his blond hair, blue eyes, and conversation sprinkled with "you-alls", he could have fooled me into thinking he was a son of the Confederacy.

All three of these gents were educated and sophisticated, the kind of clientele one would expect to run into at one of this city's more expensive hotels. They said that in addition to saving money by staying here, they enjoyed the areas set aside for social interaction and fellowship. Having taken advantage of the opportunity to talk with these interesting men over breakfast, I agreed.

After my meal, I inquired at the front desk if lockers were available for storing my luggage while I explored the city. A clerk responded affirmatively, but said I had to supply my own lock. When I didn't have any, he suggested that I buy one at the drugstore across the street. I did so, then stowed my belongings and checked out of the hostel.

Before I left for the day, a sign in the lobby for an architectural tour caught my eye. By the time I tried to join it, all spaces had been filled. Consulting a pamphlet near the front desk, I traced my own itinerary. Since the hot weather was not conducive to long stretches of hiking around the city, I bought a day's bus pass.

My first bus ride was interrupted by the whirring sounds of a ramp descending for a handicapped Afro-American passenger waiting in his motorized wheelchair. The driver slowly helped to escort him inside as the fellow maneuvered his vehicle into a special section in front where he was fastened in place. After several minutes, the other passengers were allowed to board. Two blocks away, the whole procedure was repeated in reverse, also creating a long wait. An elderly woman sitting next to me said the man was blind as well as immobile, that he rode this short course several times a week.

Feeling a mixture of compassion and annoyance, I got off the bus where Michigan Avenue crosses the Chicago River to walk along the water's edge. The heat and humidity becoming so intense, I rested on a bench to catch my breath. Surrounding me was a cityscape of architectural wonders including the stately old Wrigley building, the historic Chicago Tribune Tower, the imposing Willis (formerly Sears) Tower, and the gaudy Trump International Hotel, a glitzy edifice that didn't blend in with any of the other buildings. Nevertheless, all these uniquely designed massive structures were a visual feast.

Skyline, Chicago, IL

After craning my neck until I felt like a twisted pretzel, I resumed my walk. A half block away a film crew was shooting on the waterfront. Law enforcement had cordoned off the sidewalk skirting the waterfront. With access denied, I stood instead under the Michigan Avenue Bridge and fixed my gaze on the parade of boats passing by on the river filled with tourists. It felt like I was in Disneyland hearing the voices of the guides making their canned microphone speeches. Somebody needs to entertain visitors, but this generally is not my idea of a preferred sightseeing venue.

Crossing the bridge over to the Magnificent Mile district, I walked past several blocks of some of our nation's most expensive storefronts. Elegantly dressed and coifed business people sauntered in and out of these luxurious establishments. Many shoppers displayed the epitome of style and taste. However, a few were so ostentatious I had to keep myself from laughing. They looked like actors in a theatrical production or guests at a costume party. If you've got the money and nerve, go for it, but don't ask me to parade in one of those outfits unless you give me a strong aperitif first. I'd turn red with embarrassment in a shiny gold lamé suit, giant bow tie, and top hat.

Clock in the Loop, Downtown Chicago, IL

As I exited this high-fashionista area, lunchtime was approaching. I'd decided beforehand to patronize Gino's East, one of this city's famed pizza palaces. A Gino's franchise was located nearby next to Northwestern University. Peeking inside, I observed a wide variety of academic clientele from well-dressed professors and office workers to casually attired students. It was a great opportunity to experience some authentic Chicago pizza in a true local setting.

This busy establishment allows one to partake of an expensive stylish leisurely meal upstairs or choose to dine informally and quickly downstairs at half the price. I opted for the latter, a choice that fit in with my budget and wardrobe. While sitting at a table, I read the giant wall-to-wall chalk blackboard with its profusion of messages du jour. Scrawled on top was one item I found amusing. "I will not write on the walls" was written over and over.

As advertised, a slice of thick crust Chicago pizza with sausage, tomatoes, garlic, and cheese was ready for me to pick up at the counter in no time. While the toppings were superb, I was not particularly fond of the crust, which was heavy like coarse bread, unlike the light, crispy, thin Manhattan style I prefer. Nonetheless, the room was comfortable and the lively crowd a welcome accompaniment.

After lunch, I went to visit one of this city's outlying "resurgent neighborhoods." A guidebook had described the former Ukrainian Village as an area undergoing a comeback. It had fallen on hard times but supposedly was transitioning into streets lined with "hip" establishments. Hoping to see some old European elements and explore the new replacements, I took a subway a few miles northwest from the downtown Loop area and climbed two flights of stairs up to a concrete square in the middle of a busy intersection.

Gathered around a fenced statue in the center was a group of rowdy Afro-American youths who looked like they should have been in school at that hour. It was apparent that if there was renovation going on there, it was in its early stages. When a spaced out disheveled teenager cruised past me on a trash-filled sidewalk with a come on about buying some stuff, I got the creeps and darted for safety quickly.

A few blocks away were some interesting old brick structures, several large Victorian residences, and a large domed Eastern Orthodox Church with huge spires. Undoubtedly, this was once a proud center of Eastern European culture. I snapped a few photos, but with so many menacing characters lurking around, I saw no reason to stay. I high-tailed it back to the subway and safer environs.

My descent from the Ritz to the pits reversed, I was soon back in the Loop. The heat was so oppressive I took refuge in the Chicago Public Library. Perusing their copy of a daily newspaper, I learned that the city was in the middle of a teachers' strike and had become national news. Classes were closed and tempers were flaring. Other civic events were equally upsetting. Such is often the case in today's media.

As I was about to leave I saw a poster advertising that an expert on Middle East affairs was delivering a lecture on developments in the Arab Spring. A woman nearby seeing me read this said that the speaker was a noted man whose presentation shouldn't be missed. I was glad I had the time to attend.

At the lecture, it appeared I was in the company of some highly educated intellectuals. Among the spectators was a sprinkling of professor types. I felt like I was back in my university days. A fair number of women wearing fashionable headscarves (but no burkas) were also waiting to hear the speaker.

After a library official pleaded for financial support, he introduced the featured guest. The man walked to the podium, recited his bio as a scholar of contemporary Arab events, and pitched a short promotion of his latest book. Then he made a case for how we need to balance Western and Islamic values in dealing with the Middle East.

This articulate scholar described the revolution sweeping the region as a battle between secular democratic and traditional Islamic aspirations, warning us in Western countries to keep an open mind to both camps. He was so even-handed in his assessment of history unfolding in the area, I was impressed with his observations.

When he opened the room to questions, pandemonium broke loose. The first responder was an Israeli woman who verbally assaulted him. She screamed that Arabs hated her country, venting the same kind of anger that she was complaining about. I felt sorry for the speaker when he attempted to answer her grievances rationally to no avail. When she wouldn't stop yelling, the audience clamored for her to yield the microphone, which she gave up reluctantly.

The second responder was no better. He was a Christian evangelical who ranted about Arab terrorists and what an evil religion Islam is, just as angry in his speech as his Jewish counterpart. I know this is a touchy subject, but this sophisticated audience was subjected to such emotional tirades, I felt that I was in the middle of a Jerry Springer show. I had no interest in any more chaotic verbal brawling. With limited time before my train was to depart, I made a quick exit.

My final hour in town was spent in a hip Cuban cafe next to the hostel where I had some cutting edge Caribbean cuisine. This included a *ropa vieja* sandwich filled with black beans, plantains, and Creole spices. Afterwards, I picked up my luggage and wheeled it to the nearest bus stop where I made use of my day pass to catch the train.

At Union Station, although I arrived well ahead of departure time, there was a long line waiting to board the Amtrak **Lake Shore Limited** east. It was obvious I was not going to have the luxury of a double seat to sleep in that night. After being stuck in the queue for almost an hour, I heard an invitation over the loudspeaker for passengers over 62 to board first. Taking advantage of my senior status, I went to the front of the line.

I climbed into the coach car to which I'd been assigned, sat down and watched it fill quickly until there were no seats left. A commotion broke out when a short young Afro-American man, who looked very much like Gary Coleman, had a hissy fit about being given a seat without a window. This was a nighttime ride where there wouldn't be anything to look at, but he complained vehemently. He had such a loud and obnoxious attitude, it rankled everyone in the car.

When this impetuous youth was denied reseating, he yelled that wanted his money back. If I hadn't seen his face, his high-pitched hysterical voice sounded that of a woman. Finally, a conductor came over and told him to shut up or he'd be kicked off the train. People were muttering epithets, some that I won't repeat here.   The vibes were so thick, I expected a race riot to break out any minute. Relenting, the young guy ended his tirade with such a sour expression it would have given Bette Davis a run for her money.

By then, all I wanted was some peace and quiet. I slunk into a fetal position in my coach seat and tried to brush off this unpleasantness. When I got settled, the tall blond pony-tailed man in his late forties sitting next to me took out his computer and screen and started typing. This made me feel boxed in. It was going to be a long night.

Though I would have preferred some solitude, I tried to mitigate my discomfort by attempting to engage my new seatmate in conversation. He hailed from Sheboygan, Wisconsin. Like me, he was traveling east to visit relatives. He was full of stories about small town life that I found entertaining at first.

Then his tales of good times got more outlandish with rowdy descriptions of drunken escapades in bars, hot tubs and resort hotels. Ordinarily I wouldn't have minded this, but my energy was spent and I had trouble keeping up with his boisterous adventures. Finally, I had to ask him to open up the cyber drawbridge in front of his seat and let me out.

I took refuge in the lounge car where I hoped to unwind. After a few minutes, who would show up to keep me company but Mr. Wild Rides himself. Fortunately, he also needed to unwind from his day. His sharing became less intense, and we traded stories about moving from a larger city to a small community where people are more independent and self-reliant. Having enjoyed the transition to more personal and slower rural life styles, neither of us missed the fast lanes we once resided in. By the time we returned to our seats, I was enjoying his companionship.

Back in the coach car, the lights were dimmed. It wasn't pleasant sleeping upright in a single seat, but for a crowded venue, the place was relatively quiet. Not a snorer was heard in the whole bunch of passengers. It was also comforting to sleep near someone that in part I'd bonded with.

I know what the caged bird feels, alas!
When the sun is bright on the upward slopes,
When the wind stirs soft through the springing grass
And the river flows like a stream of glass
When the first bird sings and the first bud opes,
And the faint perfume from its chalice steals
I know what the caged bird feels

Paul Lawrence Dunbar

INDIANA TO BUFFALO
THURSDAY - SEPTEMBER 13

That evening, awkward in my semi-upright state, I dozed in fits and starts. Waking up several times in the middle of the night, I could hear other passengers also coping with their discomfort, shifting positions often. This experience was one to be muddled through.

Not only was this east coast train crowded, the vibes were intense. When daylight arrived, the Amtrak staff patrolling the car had none of the friendliness I'd experienced west of Chicago. Waking up to rust belt vistas of northwest Pennsylvania and western New York, the images of fields overgrown with weeds and littered with industrial waste were not particularly scenic. This part of my cross-country junket was one of its low points.

As we approached Buffalo, I called a rent-a-car company and asked them to send someone to meet me at the train station. I was relieved to get out of the locomotive and stretch my legs. It wasn't long before a friendly older gent signaled that he was there to escort me to the agency office. A credit card swipe and a few signed forms later, after being given the keys to an economy car I was good to go.

I drove through this non-descript neighborhood to a diner someone in the office had recommended. Eager for a big breakfast, I was disappointed to find that the place had a long waiting line inside. Perusing the menu, I thought it was somewhat pricy for standard breakfast fare. The room was so noisy my senses cried out for more peaceful surroundings. I left in search of a more comfortable, more suitable, less crowded, and less expensive eatery.

The local route into downtown Buffalo on its southern border had few restaurants along the way. None of them were to my liking, and I began to doubt my decision. Passing through a blue-collar neighborhood with long Polish surnamed taverns and small businesses, a few blocks later I noticed a cute mom-and-pop café called Trina's. Its homespun gingham curtains covering the windows called like a voluptuous siren in the culinary wilderness with a seductive "Stop here." I immediately stepped on the power brakes in my rented car and did just that.

I entered a room filled with locals that all seemed to know each other. Country music hit songs played softly in the background. As soon as I sat down, the owner, a congenial middle-aged woman, came over to my table with a hot cup of coffee and a menu with many choices.   Everything on it was considerably cheaper than the diner in the 'burbs. I knew I'd found the right place.

Someone had left a Buffalo newspaper on the table. As I read up on national and local events, a large platter filled with ham, eggs, and hotcakes that I'd ordered arrived. All were superb. An intensive read of news, weather, and sports and three more cups of coffee and I was totally satisfied. What I wanted next was to drive my temporary transport to a nearby park, find a quiet resting place, and doze off in its bucket seat. I took out a Buffalo city map and asked the café owner to recommend a tranquil spot. She pointed out Cazenovia Park about a mile away.

This was a perfect spot to unwind after such a long train ride. The lush landscaping was a sight for sore eyes. Several old buildings perked my historical interest. On my smart phone I discovered that the park had been designed by Fred Olmstead, a famous landscape architect. He created many large public areas all across the U.S., the most notable being New York's Central Park and San Francisco's Golden Gate Park.

Buffalo officials had hired Olmstead to design their system at a time when the city was one of our nation's leading urban centers. This aging metropolis may be a shadow of its former self, but its parks remain a testament to his planning and ingenuity. I took a short walk along its expanse of lawns shaded by groves of mature trees and napped contentedly in my mobile home away from home.

Irish Center, Buffalo, NY

An hour later with energy replenished, I drove into an old Irish neighborhood with several cultural centers, bars, and shops. The aged brick buildings had colorful signs that proudly displayed their Celtic heritage. These environs would make an ideal movie or sit-com locale for a show with a blue-collar theme such as "All In The Family." The streets had rows of weathered two-story residences and overgrown trees, sights not that commonly found in California.

Next, I drove downtown to see its aging architecture and survey the hostel where I'd reserved a room that night. It was in the middle of a run-down theater district where busses and light rail whizzed by. Some Broadway (off-off Broadway) productions were featured in buildings with old neon signs and rotating light bulbs that undoubtedly would be flashing later in the evening. Close by were bars and cafes for the after-the-show crowd. At mid-day, not much was happening. The hostel wasn't open until five, so I continued exploring.

Buffalo House Restaurant, Buffalo, NY

With its storied past well in decline, it is easy to see why Buffalo is not known as a tourist hot spot. Some of my friends at home asked why I even wanted to travel here. I generally find off-the-beaten-path destinations more to my liking. The word beaten describes this place to a T.

One can look at deteriorating municipal buildings for only so long. The area surrounding downtown had a third-world feel with many interesting international eateries, but several shifty-looking residents loitering on the sidewalks did not inspire a walking tour. I decided instead to visit Niagara Falls, one of the premiere U.S. tourist centers thirty miles away.

Crossing the wide, placid Niagara River over several bridges, I made my way there. The town of Niagara Falls was more charming than Buffalo and in better shape. Ethnic stores, markets, and restaurants, many with Italian surnames, lined the main thoroughfare. It came as no surprise when I discovered that this district is known as Little Italy.

I stopped for a picnic at a local park where lawn bowling was the main attraction. Behind the recreation area was a mural depicting "off the boat" Italian immigrants who traveled here carrying everything they owned on their backs as they stood on a ship taking them to America. A second mural portrayed the same family being processed at customs at Ellis Island. My Jewish grandparents on both sides of the family experienced the same at the end of the nineteenth century.

After this unexpected find, I went to the tourist area that was full of campy stores and Americana mercantilism. What I didn't expect were visitors from all over the world. Nationalities as diverse as a U.N. meeting were waiting at the entrance to a State Park that had observation points to see the falls.

There were not only numerous typical American tourists such as men decked out in gaudy Hawaiian shirts and women in frilly blouses and skirts, there were also Muslim women wearing burkas, African visitors donning patterned outfits, and Asian and Hispanic families sporting equally colorful attire. Instead of the usual hot dog and hamburger stands, there were several Indian restaurants and ethnic fast food places selling a variety of exotic snacks.

I followed the throng past the kitchy shops to the park and down several flights of stairs to a railing overlooking the falls. Though I'd seen so many images of this wide expanse of thundering water in countless books and postcards, in person these powerful cascades were (forgive the cliché) truly awesome.

The chasm separating the American and Canadian sides spans several blocks with an unbelievable amount of water flow. In the middle of the river is a huge island dividing the falls into two parts. The sounds were incredibly loud. Giant cooling mists hovered in the warm afternoon air.

Niagara Falls, NY

The city on the Ontario side is more developed than its New York counterpart. I hadn't bothered to obtain a passport card, so I had to stay in the U.S. Climbing onto a bridge rising above the river, I got a bird's eye view. At mid-week in off-season, it was overrun with onlookers. I can imagine the pandemonium at the height of summer, especially on the weekend.

After admiring the falls, I bid farewell to this dramatic passageway from Lakes Erie to Ontario. By that time, I was anticipating an authentic Polish meal somewhere in the Buffalo area. Prior research had led me to The Polish Villa, a place on the edge of town highly recommended on a local foodie website.

It was five o'clock, and the streets were gridlocked. When I finally got to the eatery, it was in the suburb of Cheektowanga (not an especially East European name), not far from where I'd rented my car earlier in the day. The restaurant was an old establishment, a bit formal for my taste. Too hungry to search for another place, I went inside. The interior reminded me of some Basque cafes I've patronized in California's San Joaquin Valley. I was seated and hoped for the best.

I skipped the huge Polish sampler plate that featured more meat than I could have digested that evening. Instead, I ordered a scaled down combination of *galumpki* (stuffed cabbage), *perogi* (a ravioli filled with sauerkraut and cheese), and potato pancakes. I enjoyed the first dish and was disappointed in the other two.

My grandmother was originally from Krakow in Southern Poland. She cooked better than these folks. The *perogi* were tasteless. I make a better potato pancake. With no spices and hardly any salt and pepper as seasoning, this was as bland a meal as I'd consumed in a while.

Although the price was fairly reasonable, I was let down. However, my young waiter was gracious. Hearing that I was from out of town, he said he also was a visitor, having traveled here from Texas to study to become a physical therapist. I told him physical therapy had been helpful when I was recovering from a back injury a few months previously and encouraged him in his goal. His interest in making my meal a pleasant one helped to mitigate my gastronomic disappointment.

Full of heavy Slavic food, I drove downtown past the neon lights to check into the hostel. This time, the place was open. For a bargain price of $25 (tax included) I was given a key and kitchen privileges. After unloading my gear in a shared room on a reserved bottom bunk bed, I went to the lounge and dining commons. A few students in the kitchen area were preparing simple fare. I took the opportunity to sit down and relax.

No sooner than I was comfortably alone at a large table in the spacious room, several people entered. A group of young German-speaking men and women seated themselves and conversed animatedly in their native tongue. I understand Spanish and can make out French to some degree, but German is Greek to me. I could only try to get the gist of their conversation by their vocal tones.

A dark-complected young man and his female companion entered and sat at the opposite end of my table, setting down some plates and a bowl of a dish they'd just prepared. When they invited me to share their meal, I declined politely, saying I'd already eaten. They wouldn't take no for an answer. I could tell that this savory concoction, a potato, tomato, and green chili omelet, was more interesting than the bland food I'd eaten earlier, so I agreed to sample a small portion.

Our food sharing opened up an immediate bond. The young man said that he was vacationing from his home in Istanbul, Turkey. His girlfriend was a Mexican-Iranian from El Paso, Texas who came here to study nursing. Although he spoke halting English, she appeared to be fluent in at least three languages. I rattled off some phrases in Spanish, but my effort to learn a few words and phrases in Turkish was not at all successful. This exotic tongue was even more foreign to me than Greek.

I asked the young man which part of Istanbul he lived in, the European or Asian side. He was surprised that an American would even know this about his hometown. I didn't let on that my knowledge was courtesy of a Google search after an earthquake hit the area the prior year. He was from the Arabic Asia Minor side and said that he'd recently earned a degree in structural engineering. I mentioned that his expertise might be valuable in a country where so many of the buildings needed retrofitting. He agreed that Turkey had a lot of work to do in this regard.

His girlfriend said Buffalo was a border city where people cross daily from Canada to shop American much like Mexicans do in El Paso. Who'd have known that these distant metropolises in upstate New York and southwest Texas would have anything in common? What a small world this large planet can be at times.

After a full day of food and conversation, I headed to my bunk bed to retire early. As in Chicago, my early bedtime placed me as the only one in the room. I needed to wake up at dawn in order to make my train. After setting my wrist-watch alarm, I prayed to the hostel gods that there wouldn't be a heavy snorer in this room that night. Falling asleep after such an eventful day was easy.

BUFFALO TO GLOUCESTER
FRIDAY - SEPTEMBER 14

Being careful not to oversleep, I awoke before my alarm sounded. As the first rays of daybreak shone through the window blinds, I was the only one up. Showering and shaving in the common bathroom, I readied myself for the road. After dropping off my key at the front desk, I drove off an hour before planned.

Seeing that there was extra time, I revisited the little café where I had eaten the day before. No sooner than I sat down, the owner came over and asked how I liked the park she'd recommended. With attentive service like this, no wonder she has such a loyal following. Not to mention the tasty home-cooked food and reasonable prices. Though I was three thousand miles away, her warm welcome made me feel right at home.

Once the car agency dropped me off at the rail station, I sat outside by the tracks and waited for a long while. After 45 minutes, many of the other passengers broke out in a chorus of complaints. A young fellow and a jolly older woman sitting next to me had a more patient attitude. We had fun mimicking the others' melodramatics.

Finally, the train arrived ATS (Amtrak Standard Time) and we boarded. I found an empty seat by a window, ready to enjoy some sightseeing. A young man sat down next to me, pulled out a huge laptop, and started entering data. After a few uncomfortable minutes, feeling like I was in someone's office, not on vacation, I changed seats. At the next stop, another cyber geek did the same thing.

There wasn't an empty seat in the coach, so I took refuge in the lounge car. I sat down at a table to decompress. Everyone but the vibrant older couple sitting across the aisle were either glued to their laptops or riveted to their headphones, oblivious to the rural upstate New York scenery. Like me, these two were enjoying the cornfields, rows of grape vines, rippling streams, deciduous forests, and rural farmhouses we were passing.

My disparagement of this sad state of human evolution didn't last long. I was interrupted by a young lady who sat herself at my table. Wishing me a "g'day," she had a thick Australian accent and had traveled here from Sydney. When I teased her about not having any electronic apparatus, she said her computer was back in her seat. She'd traveled here to see the U.S., not log onto it. I nodded in agreement. In the course of conversation, I discovered that she had a special interest in helping to protect the environment from corporations whose priorities run counter to stewardship of our planet. She considered America to be both a good and bad role model in this regard. I shared her concerns, pleased to hear that someone down under was waging the good fight to help wake up our complacent world and reverse these disturbing trends.

After the train passed the rustbelt cities of Syracuse and Utica, the tracks paralleled the Mohawk River on its approach to Albany. On both sides of this wide body of water were large rustic homes. At this time of year, the trees were beginning to turn color. In a few weeks, the region would look spectacular with its red, orange, and yellow fall foliage. I had to be content with only a preview of this phenomenon.

Meeting Of Mohawk And Hudson Rivers, Schenectady, NY

We soon crossed a series of bridges and arrived at the Albany train station. I walked inside to the desk where I was to pick up the keys to a car I'd rented.   However, there were no keys given to me, only a push button device. The agent hurriedly explained how to use it. I was so exhausted from my trip I barely heard a word the man said. He showed me where the car was parked outside and rushed off to take care of another customer.

Travel weary and dizzy from saving my appetite for a meal in Albany, it was all I could do to learn to operate this high tech car by trial and error, mostly error. After several frustrating minutes of not being able to start the car, when I finally did, it didn't run efficiently. I tried calling the agent, but got no answer. Then I contacted the front office and was referred to an 800 number for customer service where I was put on terminal hold. Ready to kick a huge dent in the fender, I eventually got through. The rep patiently gave me the quick high tech course I needed and I was on my way.

Maneuvering through thick rush hour traffic, I navigated the side streets to the highway entrance heading east towards Massachusetts. Searching for an appealing eatery, all I saw on either side of the highway were fast food establishments. When I reached the suburb of Greenbush, out of desperation I stopped at a supermarket for a stopgap snack at their salad bar. This was an effective, nutritious, and budget-friendly choice, a procedure I wound up repeating in other locations. My hunger stemmed, I drove to the upscale Berkshire community of Pittsfield an hour away looking forward to a nice dinner.

The road east was scenic, but unbelievably slow. I passed villages with low speed limit signs. All along the route I had to contend with snarls from commuters and shoppers. Drivers continually turned off the road causing delays. While gazing at the array of sprawling residences with manicured lawns and gardens, my hunger pangs returned. By the time I got to Pittsfield, I was again tired and disoriented. The only eatery in town that appealed to me was a plush-looking bistro that advertised vegan pizza. This was not my first choice, but at that point it was any port in a storm.

The restaurant was pricy, and had an upscale clientele, an extensive menu, and expensive wine list. Though the pizzas were vegan, the daily special of chicken, artichokes, and sun-dried tomatoes in a gouda cheese sauce was far from what was advertised on the sign in front. I ordered it immediately. After dining mostly in down-home places, this establishment was a delightful change. Served in a formal manner by a highly professional staff, my meal was tasty. Yet it was so rich, I could barely eat half. I requested a doggie bag, though it seemed this dish was too highbrow to feed to even the Frenchest of poodles. Somewhere later on the road east I'd be in better shape to finish it.

As I exited the café, darkness fell quickly. I drove slowly down a local highway with few signs as I approached the Massachusetts Turnpike, the route to my coastal destination. A half hour later, I found the onramp. No longer crawling at 20 miles an hour, I dodged cars speeding well over the legal limit of 65. In about the same time it took to cross the Berkshires, I traversed the whole state.

Just west of Boston, I exited the turnpike, paid my toll, and headed north on a dimly lit Interstate with confusing signage. As a Californian, I am used to well-indicated off-ramps and detailed distances to destinations up ahead. Here there were several exits for the same locale with variants that may make sense to locals, but ones that I found puzzling. Hardly any businesses and shopping centers are near the freeway to help one gauge a location. The roads here are the most challenging I've experienced anywhere in the U.S.

Finally, I reached the turnoff for Gloucester with no mention of how far it was ahead. At this late hour, all the stores and gas stations in the vicinity were closed. My car tech hadn't explained how to turn on the overhead light to read a map, so I had to wing it. When I called ahead to my friends, a delightful couple who were waiting up for me, the directions they gave were filled with traffic circles, numerous exits, and ambiguous landmarks. After an incredibly long day of travel, it took a concentrated effort to find their place. Around midnight, I finally arrived at my weekend destination.

GLOUCESTER AND CAPE ANN
SATURDAY - SEPTEMBER 15

Waking up after my first full night of sleep since leaving home, I joined one of my friends in the back of her arty-funky beach house. She was in the middle of one of her morning rituals, feeding the birds in her yard. Her summer residence is located one block from the Atlantic coast next to a marshy area where sand dunes have formed between the property and the ocean. This brackish water attracts wrens, sparrows, chickadees, and finches that enjoy feasting on the buffet of birdseeds that she lays out. Dozens of tiny warblers descended on several hanging baskets having patiently waited for their morning repast. They made a racket spreading the word that free food was available.

We went back upstairs to her patio overlooking the yard to watch the show. She pointed out the male avian visitors (the ones with the more colorful chests) and which species preferred the grub in the various feeders. The larger baskets supported the big birds, while the smaller ones had restricted landing areas which made them suitable for the tinier creatures that had trouble competing with their heftier cousins on the larger structures.

Their hearty appetites reminded us of our own hunger. She cracked open a few eggs (hopefully none of theirs) and fixed us a hearty breakfast. A whole day's activity had been planned in honor of my visit. It was a pleasure to be her passenger. I always enjoy seeing an area through the eyes of someone who lives there, so this was a great opportunity to relax and be shown around.

Our first stop was at Gloucester harbor. She'd bought two tickets for a shuttle to take us across the water to Rocky Neck, one of the most famous art colonies in Massachusetts. After a ten-minute boat ride with few passengers aboard, we stopped at the wharf on the other side of the bay. There were many cafes, galleries, and boutiques.

Nearby were the remnants of an old shipyard with a large whaling vessel perched forlornly on a roost above the harbor. One could see its tall masts where large sails once flew above and a galley with several porthole windows on the second story. Next to the ship were thick metal chains incorporated into a mechanical device that was used to transport heavy equipment on and off the boat. Just beyond the commercial district were several blocks of historic waterfront homes.

09/15/2012

Harbor Lighthouse, Gloucester, MA

An hour later, the shuttle arrived and we boarded for the return trip. This time, there were a lot more passengers. The captain gave us an extended impromptu tour accompanied by a running commentary of the history of the places we were seeing. An interesting story was how the Dogbar Breakwater got its name. He told us that it was the place where new dogs to the port were quarantined before being allowed in.

As we approached an island next to the breakwater, the tale had a twist. As part of a 4th of July celebration, the locals started a bonfire to be seen by the citizenry across the bay. They were enjoying the spectacle when it got out of control with an unintended consequence that horrified everyone. It went on to burn most of the island. Underneath the brush lived hundreds of large rats that escaped and swam to the port to avoid the flames. In a few hours, they overran the boats and homes along the shore. This launched an infestation that took months to get rid of. That'll teach the locals to play with matches.

We made another stop at a structure a hundred yards out to sea called The Greasy Pole. Once a year as part of St. Peter's Fiesta, crowds gather on the shore to watch people try to walk the length of this thirty-foot long and eight-inch wide pole lubricated for the occasion. It sticks out of what looks like a large lifeguard tower. The goal is to avoid slipping into the ocean, not an easy feat. Youtube has several videos of valiant efforts documenting this with few successes. I think it's just an excuse to drink and party onshore during and afterwards.

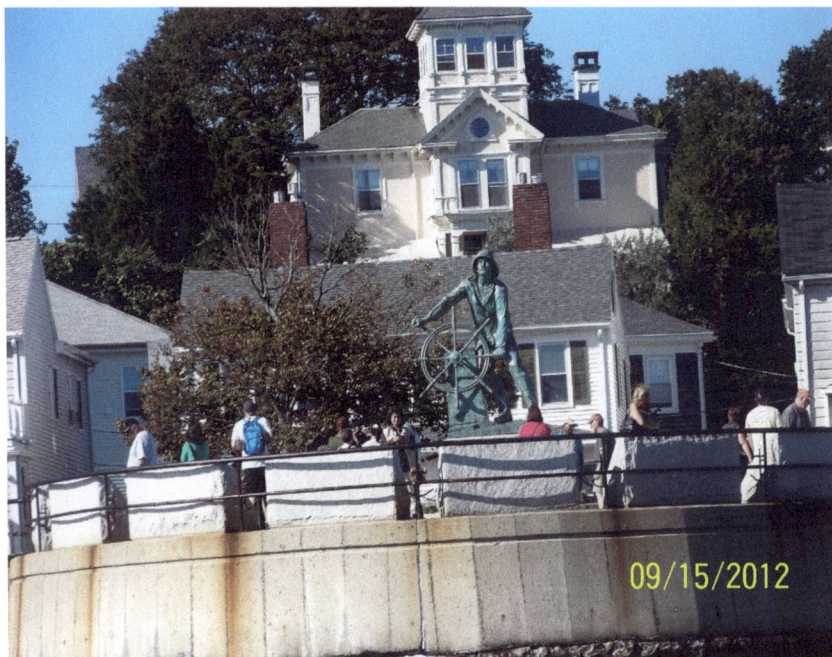

Captain Of The Wheel, Gloucester, MA

Not far from the pole was a famous statue that has become the official symbol of the city of Gloucester. The Captain Of The Wheel is a patinaed bronze portrayal of a local sailor. It is said that fifty local fisherman sat for the sculptor before he found the right model. There is no record of the name of the sailor's face incorporated into the work, a secret that followed the artist into his grave. It was a treat for us to have our boat captain's lore as part of the tour.   A final spin around the bay and we returned to the berth where we started.

We then drove to Long Beach, a stretch of sand that extends several miles to Rockport on the eastern tip of Cape Ann. On this warm end-of-summer day, the strand was full of sunbathers and people walking on the promenade. Also present were a lot of happy dog owners and their canines. September 15th is the first day dogs are allowed back in the area after being banned since mid-June for the tourist season. This was a very happy reunion for humans and animals alike.

As we approached affluent Rockport, the houses became grander. We entered the city with its art galleries, fine shops, and expensive eateries. My friend's father, when he was alive, had set up a gallery there that featured his canvasses along with several of his contemporaries. We went inside to view a tasteful collection of framed modern art. Lunch followed at a local bistro where we enjoyed a bowl of the area's signature dish, clam chowder. Seated among the city's gentrified clientele, we gazed at a spectacular view of the Rockport harbor while sampling some incredibly rich, creamy potage.

Having gotten a taste of this upper crust community, we continued on the coastal highway skirting rocky beaches and coves as the road turned north and west. On the northern shore of Cape Ann, the residences were widely scattered with large expanses of woodlands and streams running through them. Many of these houses were well over a hundred years old. Scattered every few blocks apart were picturesque cemetery plots lined with granite headstones. We stopped at one of these memorial areas that had a popular path that was used as a starting point to a spectacular overlook.

As we walked on a trail alongside a streambed my friend warned me to watch out for patches of oily dark green growth. There was poison ivy in the underbrush. Being from the west cost, I'm aware of poison oak, but this irritating plant was a new experience. I kept my hands close to my body and stepped very carefully.

After hiking through a dense deciduous forest, we arrived at a rocky bluff where we could see a great distance on this beautiful clear day. To the west there was the New Hampshire shoreline and to the northeast, a wide expanse of rocky Maine coast. The leaves on the trees were turning yellow and orange, not quite yet the famous New England red.

The sun started sinking low on the horizon. We drove to our last venue in the remaining daylight. The charming community of Annisquam is so old you'd think there would be hordes of visitors there. However, its remote location keeps this location off tourist radar. The area's historic houses dating back to the early 1800s are highly sought after, and real estate is equivalent in value to the more opulent Rockport. A short walk on a suspension bridge over a strikingly beautiful inlet filled with private boats docked in the water only added to its appeal. A colorful sunset put a final magical touch to our visit.

Back to the beach house, we took a brief rest. Her husband joined us for the evening. The plan was to go out for dinner and attend a block party in downtown Gloucester where some friends of theirs were performing. It was Saturday night on perhaps the last warm weekend of the year. All eateries were busy. We avoided the most popular ones with long waiting lines including a Portuguese bistro that I wanted to try. Instead, a nicely decorated seafood place on the harbor was where we shared a satisfying meal.

Next, we went downtown where the area was closed to traffic for an art and craft event. We had to park several blocks away. Local citizenry paraded past a variety of booths stopping to listen to singers and musicians performing various styles of folk music. Some of the restaurants had set up temporary sidewalk cafes for the occasion. Chalkboard menus lined the thoroughfare, and the tables behind them were filled with diners.

All social strata and age groups of the city were represented. Some residents were dressed formally to patronize the high-end restaurants, while others were outfitted more casually in t-shirts, shorts and sandals. Couples strolled by holding hands, seniors ambled along with canes, and youngsters chased each other playfully. After listening to my friend's friends perform a variety of traditional American folk tunes, we capped the evening at an ice cream parlor decorated with retro posters of Hollywood notables such as Marilyn Monroe, Rock Hudson, Steve McQueen, and James Dean.

GLOUCESTER TO FALL RIVER
SUNDAY - SEPTEMBER 16

The next morning I once again joined my hostess in her bird feeding ritual. Little did these creatures know that this was to be their last hurrah. My friends were packing up to return to the west coast. A few rabbits and chipmunks feasted on tidbits that fell from the feeders.

After breakfast, my hosts showed me Good Harbor Beach a few blocks from their residence. Sun worshippers were getting in some of the season's last licks. A picturesque well-weathered old hotel fronted the beach. The warm humid air and gentle Atlantic waves felt completely different from my familiar Pacific shoreline where the water, contrary to its tranquil name, is seldom gentle.

Thanking my friends for their gracious hospitality, I bid farewell and drove off to explore New England. My first destination was Salem with its historic buildings, witch museums, and famed waterfront harbor. Some of the attractions were a bit campy for my taste, especially the witch houses. However, seeing some of the centuries-old boats in the harbor alone was worth the stop here. I wasn't prepared for the throngs of people with the same goal. Caught in a gridlock of gawking visitors, I walked quickly around the central district and old port and drove away searching for quieter surroundings.

The first city I came to was the charming town of Mapleton. It was similar to places I'd seen on Cape Anne. The sprawling mansions were attractive, the old trees lining the streets were lovely, and the large established landscaped gardens a real treat. But I was more interested in visiting the less manicured areas in Southern Massachusetts on my way to Rhode Island.

The highway signage didn't improve as I headed south. Finding a gas station and place to eat was as challenging as spelling Massachusetts correctly. Most commercial centers were situated a long distance from the highway offramps. Several franchised restaurants were not to my liking, so I settled for a grocery store salad bar picnic instead. Surprisingly, this turned out to be a very healthful, economical, and satisfying choice.

An hour down the road was the industrial town of Fall River, a quaint city rich in history that has seen better days. It was a welcome antidote to so many tourists up north. Distinctive old churches and antique Victorian residences were perched on hills overlooking Narragansett Bay. Bridges hovering over this large body of water made a spectacular backdrop.

09/16/2012

Steel bridge over Narragansett Bay, Fall River, MA

This late in the afternoon, many of the locals were sitting on their balconies or walking along the hills to observe the last rays of sunlight highlighting the tall ships below. After joining the walkers for a short hike and savoring the sights, I took a drive through town.

Braga Bridge Frames Downtown Fall River, MA

An aspect of Fall River that surprised me was its prevalence of Portuguese stores and restaurants. Few pockets of this ethnicity are found on the west coat. What remains has blended into the mainstream. I wanted to sample a Portuguese café, but having just eaten, I wasn't hungry. So I continued on to Rhode Island.

Sound, Providence, RI

About 20 miles to the west, I turned off the highway just inside the capital city of Providence, home to Brown University and the Rhode Island School Of Design (RISD), well-regarded higher educational institutions I wanted to visit. I felt comfortable in this academic community with its stately homes, ethnic cafes, and sophisticated boutiques. Students and other academic types were scurrying to and fro on the sidewalks. One-of-a-kind shops, bookstores, and coffee houses were filled with customers. It reminded me of my college days at UCLA in Westwood Village and many visits to UC Berkeley where my friends and I patronized establishments like these.

Nearing dinnertime, I was ready for a culinary adventure, hopefully Portuguese. An array of ethnic possibilities piqued my curiosity, but none were from Portugal. I chose Ethiopian, a cuisine one doesn't run into very often. Since this eatery was completely full, the help seated me at a lonely table out on the sidewalk. After almost a half hour of being stranded without anyone giving me a menu or taking my order, I consulted my smart phone for another interesting place to try. I remembered an Italian café I'd seen in a guidebook in the suburb of Cranston on the other side of the city and decided to go there instead.

Student commercial district, Providence, RI

Old houses in academic neighborhood, Providence, RI

On the way there I took a drive through downtown Providence. Although this delightful city had intriguing galleries and establishments, there was no place to park without a high price tag. Not willing to pay double digits to facilitate a short walking tour, I had to acquaint my self with merely a quick drive-though.

I headed for Cranston, just west of town. It turned out to be disappointedly noisy, dirty, and poorly lighted, not at all what I'd hoped to experience. A downside in relying on guides and recommendations is that one has no idea of selection's setting. The gummed up traffic and long red light signals on every block only added insult to injury.

I was hoping that the Italian restaurant might make up for this poor choice of locale, but as luck would have it, the place was closed that day. By then, the hour was getting late and on a weekday evening my choices were diminishing. In desperation, I tried my phone again. This time I found a (sigh) Portuguese restaurant in East Providence close to where I'd been previously. My instincts had been on target earlier, even if my timing was not.

With closing hour approaching, I made a phone call to reserve a table. The hospitable hostess assured me that the bar stayed open late and the help would be happy to accommodate an out-of-towner, even if the clock ran a little over. I followed her directions to an industrial district where a large old-fashioned upscale building seemed out of place in its dilapidated surroundings. Seemingly in the middle of nowhere, the eatery was full of customers, mostly sitting at the bar.

As soon as I was seated in the dining room, the friendly waiter handed me a menu and placed a basket of freshly baked Portuguese sourdough bread on the table. After gratefully downing a slice, I ordered a chicken dish cooked in a white wine sauce with artichokes, pimentos, and fresh basil. It was brought on a platter large enough to serve a family of four. This entree was ample and well-prepared. I couldn't have been more pleased.

While I was dining, a stocky, olive-skinned man in his 50s escorted a smartly dressed black woman half his age to a table near me. I tried not to be judgmental, but was tempted to think of this "dinner date" as something on the sordid side. However, when the two conversed warmly in Portuguese, my imaginary Mafia-style movie came to a screeching halt. My friends in Gloucester had told me that many Portuguese immigrants in New England are from the Azores. I quickly snapped my inquiring mind back into silence.

I shifted my focus to the delicious meal in front of me. It was so huge I could barely eat one-third of what had been served. I asked my waiter for a doggie bag. A kennel-sized container would have been more in order. I could look forward to an extra meal or two in the near future.

Next on my agenda was a reasonably priced motel. I stopped at a few colorful, or better put, off-colorful places on the business highway loop heading east. Pulling into their parking lots gave me the creeps. I did inquire about rates at some offices, but the grounds looked so seedy, I was afraid something dangerous might occur there.

Consulting my phone for a safer sanctuary, I found a Motel 6 just over the Massachusetts border in Skekonk. When I phoned to ask for directions, an indifferent desk clerk spit out a long list of streets and turnoffs. I tried following them but got lost. Calling her for assistance a few times, the instructions did not improve with repetition.

After several false moves, I finally found the place and went in to register, ready to complain about her poor guidance. By then, a new desk clerk had taken over the helm. She was as nice as the other one had been surly. She apologized profusely saying that this location had confounded many patrons. When I asked for a senior discount, she said she didn't believe I was old enough for it. Imagine, being carded just a few days before I was about to turn the age of 66. That certainly made my day.

I was given a key to a small welcoming suite that recently had been redecorated in a cheerful modern style. Everything was new and worked perfectly. The bed was firm and comfortable and the TV had over 100 stations, including one in Portuguese. I watched with avid interest as great moments in this country's history were interspersed with current happenings in the local community. I especially enjoyed the vignettes of explorers who brought glory to Portugal such as Vasco Di Gama and Bartholomew Diaz. That night, I fell asleep counting Portuguese sheep and dreamt of riding in big wooden ships on conquests of Africa and Asia.

We were tired, we were very merry
We had gone back and forth on the ferry,
It was bare and bright, and smelled like a table
We lay on a hilltop underneath the moon
And the whistles kept blowing, and the dawn came soon

Edna St Vincent Millay

FALL RIVER TO NEW LONDON
MONDAY - SEPTEMBER 17

Since I was halfway back to Fall River, the next morning I decided to revisit the place. Just north of downtown was a district of historic churches of many denominations including an old Jewish temple with rounded domes that evoked a Renaissance style. This building's faded yellow-green and tangerine colors were unlike the somber gray granite of the other houses of worship. Perhaps this place had some Sephardic members. I can just see Christopher Columbus sneaking out of a service not at all eager to reveal his partial Jewish heritage. If the folks north of here at Salem would have found this out, he might have been persecuted as a heretic. I can only hope that whatever happens in Fall River, stays in Fall River.

I came upon a little café called George's on a residential side street, an unusual place for a restaurant. Not one to pass by an intriguing mom 'n pop cafe, I ventured in to see a long counter and a few tables with shiny plastic tablecloths. Before I could sit down, the owner came out of the kitchen wearing a chef's hat and apron, a character in a place with equal character. The room was clean and funky, qualities that easily win my patronage.

"George" welcomed me with a menu and a hot cup of coffee, asking if I was a local. When I told him I was from California, he shared that he'd run a food truck in Thousand Oaks, a suburb northwest of LA. This started a lively conversation. While preparing my breakfast he recounted his experiences skating around government regulations that had made his meals on wheels business very challenging. After only eking out a living for several years, he returned to his native city to open this cafe a week ago. I was one of his first customers.

He brought me a simple meal of eggs and home fried potatoes with a Mediterranean flair. When I asked him why there were so many churches here with signs in Portuguese, he explained that over 30% of Fall River's population is of Portuguese descent. He reinforced what I'd heard about Azorean influence when he stated that half of the recent immigrants here are from the islands. Seeing how much I was enjoying his food, he treated me to a sample of a local favorite, *linguica*, Portuguese sausage, which was very tasty. We discussed the rewards and pitfalls of starting a small business.

I was his lone diner for a half-hour until a new person came in, a health worker here for a second visit. He related to George some of his nutritional concerns. Then a portly gentleman entered with a slim woman and a red-haired boy. They all talked sports, especially the fate of the New England Patriots. Then the conversation changed to diet and exercise, the health worker advising the man to shed a few pounds. When this big guy got defensive, George diplomatically diffused the situation. A talented chameleon able to sense his customers' needs, he seemed to have what it takes to establish a successful business. If I lived here, I'd certainly be a regular.

Afterwards, I drove through downtown to check out several Portuguese businesses. This was truly "Little Portugal," a moniker that Fall River often wears. These included a large tapas bar, a social club, and a liquor bar, all with corresponding ethnic surnames. The area seems to be thriving. As much as I tried, it was impossible to find a parking place anywhere nearby.

Following this cursory exploration, I crossed the large steel bridge back into Rhode Island and this time got off the freeway a little earlier. This allowed me to explore the city of East Providence. Observing many unusual stores, markets, bakeries, and restaurants that unfortunately I didn't have time to investigate, I sighed and returned to the area surrounding the university. I lamented, "So many sights and so little time."

After admiring more academic and residential buildings, I discovered a local bakery. I succumbed to my impulses and went inside to buy some road snacks. This artisan establishment had a large display of freshly baked pastries, scones, muffins, and breads. They looked so inviting I wanted to buy out the whole store. The voice of George's health worker kept repeating in my head, so I limited my purchases to a few items. Eavesdropping can help mitigate a bad habit. If this bakery were near my home, I'd need great willpower to keep from gaining several pounds.

Heading west, I drove through downtown Providence and browsed its galleries featuring contemporary paintings, graphics, and collages. Wall after wall featured displays of high quality artwork in a variety of styles. This highly artistic community is geared for those with much larger budgets than mine, so it was strictly a look but don't even think of buying experience.

West of this capital city, the freeways were filled with traffic in the early afternoon. No stranger to gridlock, I patiently made my way out of the congestion as soon as was possible. Finally, the traffic thinned, and I entered a more rural area. A "pick your own apples" sign motivated me to follow a winding road through prosperous old country homes and farmhouses. I arrived at a large expanse of cornfields and orchards. Driving into a parking lot next to a tented produce store, I went inside to investigate.

Rows of canned goods and a rack of pick-your-own bags were displayed in front of a cashier stand. When I asked the woman behind the register about the picking procedure, she handed me a bag, advising that a full one would probably run me around $15.

I walked over to where hundreds of trees were loaded with red and green apples with many hues in between. The rows were labeled with one of eight varieties available, and most were ready to harvest. I picked enough for my travel needs and plenty to give as gifts to the relatives I was scheduled to visit in the coming days. A half bag was more than sufficient.

Back at the store, I saw an old man, the orchard's patriarch. I asked him why his globes were so large while my trees at home had small clusters of fruit. He replied that this was probably due to the nature of the blooms. Single blooms produce large fruit while multiple blooms need to be thinned out. Being a neophyte in this area, I had a lot to learn. Thanking him for his insight, I paid for my efforts. Returning to my car, I ate one of the sweetest apples I'd ever tasted, feeling better about this purchase than the pastries I'd consumed earlier.

Continuing westward, I made it to the Connecticut border in no time. The state of Rhode Island is so tiny one can cross it quickly. At first, the other side of the border looked the same. But when I pulled off the road to make a phone call, I found myself in a neighborhood of modest modular homes on raised foundations, a far cry from the stately mansions I'd just visited.

Continuing south along a state highway, I saw a sign for Hopeville Road State Park that inspired me to take a rest. In typical New England fashion, there was no indication how far down the road the site was located. I drove past a pastoral community of older homes under large spreading trees. After quite a few miles I arrived at a stunning body of water with several picnic tables by its shoreline. It was a promising place to stop and recharge.

Only two other people were in the park, one of them sunbathing on a blanket and the other wading in hip boots inside the lake. I thought he was trolling for biological specimens, but when I asked what he was doing, his reply surprised me. He was using a metal detector to hunt for coins and jewelry that had fallen into the water. So far his day's catch was seventeen cents, not even close to minimum wage. I wished him luck and shifted my attention to the natural beauty around me.

The sun was warm and the water placid as migrating birds passed overhead. Fish jumped out of the water while a slight breeze skirted through the leaves of the trees. This may not have been Walden Pond, but Hopeville was an apt name for such a peaceful place.

Getting hungry again, I needed to leave. Then I remembered the Portuguese dinner I'd packed in the car from the night before. I sat myself down at a picnic table and enjoyed a fantastic meal by the water's edge. As often is the case with leftovers, the flavors had improved overnight. While I dined, several large birds flew by making ripples in the lake every time they dove into the water. I could have lingered in this blissful spot for quite a while longer, but I wanted to travel farther and perhaps get close to Long Island Sound before I stopped for the night.

Back on the Interstate, the highway wove through a verdant region of forests and streams. Unlike California, the roadways here have no billboards to interfere with the natural surroundings. This makes travel more aesthetic, but also a little boring. Being from afar, I like to read about attractions and businesses that lie ahead and get a sense of local character. Yet it was pleasant not to be inundated with advertising and able to witness this natural setting undisturbed.

By the time I approached the city of Norwich, I was ready for some sightseeing, coffee, and dessert. Once again, the road signs were confusing. I meandered through outlying areas of town filled with elegant old houses. This soon gave way to a rougher working-class neighborhood with much smaller structures. The sudden change of social strata was a pattern I was to encounter often in Eastern Connecticut.

Downtown Norwich has many funky bars and little shops. There were more motorcycles parked on the street than cars. At 6pm, most of the places had shut down, including Dunkin Donuts, which was closed by the time I arrived. No coffee bars were open either. I couldn't find a decent place to stop for a snack other than a park across from a sewage treatment plant on the river that ran through the city. This was not my idea of a welcome respite from driving.

I continued to the interstate and settled for a fast food franchise stop, a nondescript burger place where the locals were hanging out. This gave me a chance to eavesdrop on some chatter. However, there was nothing special in anyone's conversation and nothing distinctively regional about the food or the environs. I could have been in any city or state.

Not inspired to stay in this nondescript area overnight, I continued south. A smart phone search revealed inexpensive accommodations along the way. Not that far down the highway in the town of Nyacit was a Motel 6. This franchise had worked so well the previous night I hoped to repeat the experience. Though redecorated in the same style, its infrastructure was in bad shape, the facilities poorly maintained, the room was near a lot of traffic, and the television had a limited selection of stations. For a cheap stay, I would have preferred a youth hostel, but as far as I knew, Connecticut had none. It was any port in a storm. I'd rate this establishment a Motel 5 at best.

I made a final meal out of the remainder of my Portuguese leftovers, watched a couple of TV programs, and called it a day. This inhospitable motel room with its thin walls and ceilings combined with some noisy neighbors kept me tossing and turning all night. I hoped that the next day would produce better results.

There is something that sets the gypsy blood astir;
We must rise and follow here,
When from every hill of flame
She calls and calls each vagabond by name

Bliss Carmen

NEW LONDON TO ALBANY
TUESDAY - SEPTEMBER 18

I hit the road early the next morning and followed a local route to New London, a city not that far away that I knew nothing about. Sometimes it is good to travel without expectations. With nothing to guide me, I had to follow my hunches. A series of rundown streets with disheveled movie theaters and liquor shops euphemistically called "package stores" led me to a scenic shoreline drive. There was a waterfront district with small boats moored in the docks along the coast. Passing a neighborhood of old houses in various states of neglect, I stopped to view Eugene O'Neill's prior summer home, a historically preserved rustic wooden structure with a pleasant view of the inlet sea.

Eager for a good breakfast, I searched for an eatery. The only one I found was a funky seafood stand called Fred's Shanty. They didn't serve breakfast, so I drove on. I stumbled on an old building called Fort Trumbull. This antique fortress overlooking the harbor had a massive stone structure and rows of cannons pointed to intercept approaching ships.

I was in the middle of taking a photo of this imposing building when a couple walked into my shot. They apologized profusely. Thanking them for giving it a sense of scale, I was surprised to find that they were locals visiting the fort for the first time. Since they lived in the area, I asked them for a breakfast recommendation. They couldn't name any, but for a good meal I should try a seafood shanty down the road. It had to be Fred's. Since by then it was approaching noon, I decided to kiss off breakfast and have lunch there instead.

This proved to be wise. I ordered a bowl of clam chowder that was even tastier than what was served in the expensive Rockport bistro a couple of days earlier. A savory sandwich of freshly caught fish with all the trimmings was also excellent. From my bench on the outdoor patio, the harbor view was delightful. I hit a home run at this waterfront café.

Someone had left a local newspaper on my table. Reading through it I learned that the Norwich-New London area had suffered during the economic slump of the past few years. Real estate prices had fallen compared to the more affluent western part of the state. This helped explain the patchwork quilt of neighborhoods I'd seen. Downtown New London, though colorful, had seen better days. An appealing dining spot was nowhere to be seen. What shops that remained looked like they were hanging on for dear life.

Fort Trumbull, New London, CT

Downtown New London, CT

It was time to head north toward Albany where I'd made plans to stay with relatives. A series of local roads led me into a region of country manors surrounded by woods and large ponds. The sorry environs near the coast were soon just a memory. Rural homesteads lined with signs selling fresh produce and eggs were prevalent.

My next destination was Hartford, the state capitol. It proved to be as bland a governmental center as Providence, Rhode Island is colorful. It began to rain hard, so I waited out the storm in a tree-lined park on the shores of the Hartford River. In the distance I could see many municipal buildings downtown. The skyline was unremarkable, but the torrential rain falling on the hood of my car as the river rolled by was memorable. During this hour of unrelenting precipitation I used the time to catch up on my reading.

Before leaving the area, I'd promised a friend near home who once lived here that I'd visit Miss Porter's School For Girls, a place we often joked about. Located in Farmington, one of Hartford's wealthier suburbs, for decades this finishing school has attracted young teenagers who aspire to attend Ivy League universities and have their sights set on marrying well. Such an institution is unheard of on the libertarian west coast where etiquette is not as highly valued.

Blue blood does not flow through my veins, and I'm certainly not a candidate to attend this upright institution.   Neither Harvard nor Yale are on my radar, and I don't entertain the notion of marrying into money. Yet I was interested in seeing how the other half lives. Curtailing this curiosity, the heavy rain precluded an extended visit.   So I saluted he future Stepford wives of America and high-tailed it out of there.

Back in my car, I turned on the radio to hear that not only was the region being pelted by heavy rainfall, there were also tornado warnings, rare for this part of the U.S. Driving slowly and carefully, I gingerly approached the northwestern part of this little state.

When the rain finally abated, I stopped for a beverage break at a McDonald's franchise in a remote town just outside of New Canaan. After ordering a senior coffee, I noticed a table of local oldsters who had done the same. I used this as a pretext to engage them in conversation. A mutual appreciation of our bargain beverage formed a bond. They welcomed me to join them.

These colorful gents were surprised to learn that I was from California. Few visitors from afar ever stop in their hamlet. When I inquired if they liked living there, an oldster with a thick Yankee accent said it was a difficult question to answer because he'd never lived anywhere else and had nothing to compare it to. Most of them had hardly traveled any distance from their sleepy village. I confessed that I was glad to have left a big city's frustrations for a small town out west. I doubt if they understood what I was talking about, not having ever experienced crowds and congestion. Who knows if ignorance can be considered to be bliss, but I sensed that they seemed to be content with their lot.

At the next highway junction, I entered the town of North Canaan. Its old movie theater, historic churches, and vintage used car lot made me feel that I was in a time warp. I wanted to explore this city full of nostalgic signs and sights, but I had a destination to reach and time was running out.

Turning north, I crossed the border back into Massachusetts. The hick town ambiance immediately gave way into upscale mansions and gentleman farms. This was the well-heeled Berkshire region I'd heard much about. These upscale cities had the type of fancy shops and steak houses popular a few decades ago. Opulent imported cars were parked in front of these swanky establishments.

Shops, Stockbridge, MA

When I got to Stockbridge, I couldn't find an entrance to the Interstate. The lack of helpful highway directions was again a problem. I pulled into a parking lot of a swanky bistro to consult a map. A group of patrons exiting from a luxury sedan walked by me with their noses turned up. They seemed aghast at my late model push-button Nissan Sentra, a poor cousin compared to their plush modes of transport. In their silk suits and ties, designer dresses, jewelry, and furs, they sauntered like gaudy colored waterfowl, looking askance at my "ugly duckling." Imagine, if I'd been parked there in my old pickup truck, I might have caused a scandal or been run out of town.

A sign pointed to a westward entrance to the turnpike. I drove twenty miles on a frontage road that paralleled the highway without seeing one. Not until I crossed the New York state line was there any onramp. It was as if the region's Department of Transportation's motto to visitors was "Welcome to our area, now go home."

Finally on the interstate, I was able to make up some time. As I approached Albany, there was more confusing signage.   I called my cousin to get the right directions. I still made a few wrong turns. How lucky I am to live in a state that knows how to direct traffic.

My relatives welcomed me with open arms and a home cooked dinner. Afterwards, I settled in for the night. Sleep came easy after a long adventurous day.

ALBANY AND TROY
WEDNESDAY - SEPTEMBER 19

The next morning, my hosts asked what I'd like to do that day. I responded, "as little as possible." I needed some down time. They were relieved since they had scheduled a few activities on their own.

After a relaxing morning, I had enough energy by late afternoon to explore the area in my rental car. Since I was already familiar with Albany from prior visits, I asked what they thought I might find of interest. They recommended the historic architecture in downtown Troy across the Hudson River. The area was in the process of rehab from a period of decay with many new entrepreneurial establishments worth taking a look at.

Driving my high-tech car to this low-tech destination, the area lived up their description. Downtown Troy has many stately old office buildings, venerable brownstone waterfront apartments, and a variety of unique artisan shops. A walk through the city center led me past an old movie theater that harkens back to bygone days with antique lettering and design. Some of these structures looked suitable for a movie shoot, a project with a northern equivalent of a decadent Tennessee Williams southern play.

Amidst these relics, 2012 was in the air, at least on the airwaves. Older autos cruised the area blasting rap music on loud car stereos almost to the point of shattering my eardrums with their high decibel levels. Accompanying this annoyance were sidewalks filled with ne'er-do-well appearing young men, most of them white, some Afro-American. I needed to watch my back.

Situated on some of the seedier streets were several trendy high-priced adventurous cafes that were frequented by young hipsters. I passed an appealing Greek restaurant, but was not in a position to sample it because my cousin had already invited me for dinner. I scrawled down the address, hoping that she and her husband would try it out for me at a later time.

Downtown Troy, NY

Another find was a vegan bakery where I bought some non-dairy creamy pastries to share with my hosts. These expensive desserts were a letdown. Baking without butter or eggs requires special talents that many vegan entrepreneurs possess, but not these merchants. They may not have mistreated any animals, but my taste buds and wallet felt abused. My cousin and her husband treated me to a wonderful non-vegan charbroiled steak dinner that more than made up for my disappointing dessert.

It was good to sit with my relatives and catch up on family matters. After watching more TV shows with them, I bid the world farewell and slept soundly in their comfortable peaceful suburban residence.

Hipster district, Troy, NY

As long ago they raced,
Last night they raced again
I heard them inside me,
I felt the roll of the land

I think I will remember now
Until the end of the world
How lordly were the straightaways,
How lyrical the curves

Mark Van Doren

ALBANY TO PEEKSKILL
THURSDAY - SEPTEMBER 20

After a tasty bagel, lox, and cream cheese breakfast, I said goodbye to my hosts and drove to the Amtrak station where I returned my rented car and boarded an **Empire Service** train south.   My destination was Croton-On-Hudson, just outside of Peekskill where another cousin was waiting for my arrival. On this uneventful ride, as the tracks paralleled the Hudson the views of the river were obscured. Occasionally, the foliage thinned out and I could see a wide expanse of water with large mansions perched above the cliffs on the other side. Many of these residences were vacation homes of influential people, well-to-do families like the Astors and Rockefellers.

At Croton, my cousin was indeed waiting for me. We drove to her cottage in Peekskill where her husband and three dogs greeted me. The oldest canine I'd met previously, the two younger ones being new additions. Both of these had glad-to-see-you-now-go-home conflicts. The youngest was very cute, but growled anytime I got too close. I named her "Doggie Dearest" because of her tendency to snap for no apparent reason. Rescued from a shelter where she'd been subjected to abuse, I saw how much she wanted to be loved, yet was insecure about receiving what she needed. Not having the energy for this high maintenance challenge, I took refuge in the guest room and tried to get some rest.

Later that day we went to downtown Peekskill for an Italian dinner. I was hoping to experience a traditional east coast ethnic café with red-and-white-checked tablecloths, travel posters from Italian cities, and melted candle drippings over old wine bottle holders. The place we went to had none of this. However, the menu was on target and the food was excellent. Italian songs and opera arias played in the background and pungent smells of garlic and cheese wafted in from the kitchen. When I closed my eyes I tried to pretend that I was in my desired atmosphere, not a beige modern eatery. We finished our dinners with enough leftovers for a second meal later. A short driving tour of downtown Peekskill after our meal was followed by a return to their welcoming home and not as welcoming canines.

Downtown Peekskill, NY

Like the night before, I retreated quickly to the spare bedroom to avoid any doggie dramatics. I had no need to count sheep or German shepherds to fall asleep. I was tired, dog tired.

I am of old and young, of the foolish as much as the wise,
Regardless of others, ever regardful of others,
Maternal as well as paternal, a child as well as a man,
Stuff'd with the stuff that is coarse
and stuff'd with the stuff that is fine.

Walt Whitman

PEEKSKILL AND NEW YORK CITY
FRIDAY - SEPTEMBER 21

After serving a healthy breakfast of fruits nuts, granola, and herbal tea, my cousin invited me to accompany her to meet a local artist friend of hers. We drove to a wooded area where this gifted man had a rustic cabin surrounded by hundreds of sculptures and mobiles.

He is a holocaust survivor who has expressed his experiences in his artwork. Before showing us anything, he related the story of how as a teenager he was imprisoned by the Nazis in Hungary. He escaped only to be captured by Russian Guards in the Ukraine soon afterwards. Once again he managed to free himself. This time, he found safe haven with western troops.

After the war ended, he took refuge in the British protectorate in Cyprus and later emigrated to Israel. In this newly established Jewish state he became a conscript in the army. After his service, he studied psychiatry and worked in the field for a while before resettling in the U.S.

This amazingly productive man led us on a tour of dozens of his original sculptures, some serious and some comic. They were perched on pedestals in his outdoor garden. Then he took us inside his house to show us a large folder filled with illustrations of the life he endured in the prison camps. Included on each page was a caption describing one horror after another. He hopes to publish a collection of these someday as a book. Both his artwork and his life story were very impressive. I wished him the best in finding the recognition he truly deserves.

Later that afternoon, my cousin and I got ready to go to Manhattan where she, a talented painter in her own right, was participating in a woman's art association gallery exhibit in Soho. She put on some fine clothes while I upgraded my wardrobe from T-shirt to polo shirt, the best I could do with my limited selection. She assured me that anything goes in today's art scene.

We took a local train south into the city. It was late in the afternoon and the car was so crowded, we had to sit separately. I was enjoying the rural scenery along the Hudson but it soon gave way to an increasingly urban landscape. By the time we reached Yonkers, the populated areas were very dense.

Our first city stop was Harlem, once an Afro-American ghetto. I had always thought of this borough as a depressed area. Today, it is anything but, very upscale due to recent gentrification. In all directions I saw blocks of cafes and shops bustling with activity.

The train's next stop was Yankee Stadium where half the passengers got off to see a baseball game held that day. Not particularly a Yankee fan myself, I couldn't help but sense the intense anticipation of this crowd of people sporting athletic regalia imprinted with their team's insignias.

Those of us remaining on the train were quickly whisked underground, the vista of tall buildings soon replaced by dimly lit cement pilings and parallel rows of dingy railroad tracks. It was only a short hop to downtown Manhattan. By the time we reached the end of the line, the tracks joined a myriad of distinct tracks each with its own separate landing platform for incoming and departing passengers.

I followed my cousin onto a skinny boarding area and walked two long blocks into Grand Central Station. It was 5:30, the middle of rush hour. Crowds of people scurried to and fro. On the south wall of this immense room with an incredibly high ceiling was a schedule of trains, destinations, and boarding areas. In the middle was a large round sculptured clock on top of a pedestal that is often used a meeting place for relatives and friends. None of the urban scenarios I'd visited thus far prepared me for the frantic activity of such a onrushing mass of humanity. It was truly a culture shock.

Grand Central Station, NY, NY

Out on the street, which was even more crowded than the train station, we took a staircase a few flights down to the subway where we boarded a car to the Village. Since no seats were available, we had to stand holding onto straps for dear life. The rickety vehicle shook us in every direction. Every strata of Manhattan society surrounded us including executives in expensive business suits, immigrants in rags, jocks in outfits with team logos, and rap aficianados listening to headphones and dancing in place.

Manhattan Street Scene, NY, NY

After a few stops where literally hundreds of people got on and off the car, we climbed up to a street where more crowds were milling about. As it approached twilight, streetlights and neon signs began to light up the area. Sidewalks full of litter, pedestrians ignoring traffic lights, and horns honking in abundance are the images I remember most. We made our way past rows of commercial buildings, corner storefronts, and a series of construction zones that had temporary plywood fencing around them.

The gallery building was hidden behind one of these plywood structures. Once inside, we got in line to wait for an elevator that did not inspire confidence. It was so rickety that many Catholics must cross themselves in transit as it slowly creaks its way up. Having no religious signature for protection, I instead made a silent prayer to the universe to see us up to the fourth floor unscathed.

When the elevator doors and iron grate opened, my call for devine intervention was answered. We entered a large room buzzing with activity and a diverse crowd. The exhibit featured the creations of Greater New York City female visual artists in various media and styles. Hundreds of framed artworks were hung on the walls, one from each member of this woman's group. A lovely seascape painted by my cousin was among those on display. On one side of the room was a temporary bar where a well-dressed middle-aged Afro-American man served small glasses of white wine and champagne (I imagine red wine would have stained the carpeting).

My cousin introduced me to some fellow artists. It wasn't long before she got caught up in conversation with her friends. I took the opportunity to go on my own to take in the imagery. The majority of these works were unique in style and presentation. As is the case with creative efforts, I found some more to my liking than others. In general, I felt that there was high level of skill and talent.

I sat down to rest on a chair in the middle of the room and struck up a conversation with an engaging woman a little older than me. She'd just returned to art after a career as a book publisher. Just as I was picking her brain for some tips on marketing, it was announced that ribbons and cash prizes were going to be awarded to several members. We happened to be sitting right in front of the action.

At first, I was excited to be situated so close. But after about thirty awards were granted, followed by long grateful acceptance speeches and polite applause, half of the prizes were yet to be handed out. For the artists involved, I'm sure that these were welcome acknowledgements, but the two of us rolled our eyes at each other with "enough already" expressions on our faces.

Finally, the parade of awards and speeches were finished. Unfortunately, my cousin's name wasn't called. Like cheering up a jilted sports fan, I tried to encourage her with "maybe next year" and a pat on the back. We went over to the bar to mitigate our disappointment with another small glass of wine and a few tasty hors d'oeuvres. I limited my consumption of these tidbits because I knew we were going out for dinner afterwards and didn't want to spoil the adventure.

As I'd anticipated, I was invited to accompany my cousin and her colleagues out for a meal. They chose to dine at a Ukrainian restaurant in the Village, which sounded fine to me. However, we walked so fast I didn't have time to take in the neighborhood. I learned that evening the meaning of a New York minute. As much as I wanted to fully observe the people, sights, and shops of this section of the Big Apple, it was pretty much all a blur.

At the eatery there was a long line and resulting wait. I was sorry I hadn't eaten a few more of those free snacks. Once seated at a table in a room of artistic types like us, we were served similar dishes to the ones I'd ordered in the Polish eatery in Buffalo. This time, the food was much better prepared. Sharing this repast in the company of bohemian comrades made it even more enjoyable.

Unlike the wildly expensive Manhattan dining scene, this establishment was reasonable, about the same price as the Buffalo eatery. The portions were so large, my "doggie bag" had enough contents for another whole meal the next day.

Manhattan Street Scene At Night, NY, NY

On the train ride home, my cousin was so tired from her long day, she fell asleep in her seat.   I can imagine the energy it takes to prepare for such an event and to be "on" while socializing. She missed seeing the hordes of baseball fans get on the train at Yankee Stadium. The home team must have won because everyone had big smiles on their faces. Young folks in pin-striped clothing were high-fiving each other, loudly boasting how the Bronx Bombers played that night. My hopes for a quiet ride home dashed, I envied my cousin's repose.

Back at her house, "Doggie Dearest" began to get on my nerves again. But this time I tried to calm her agitation by giving her a piece of a Ukrainian sausage from my leftovers. Missing my affectionate pooch at home, I remembered how a treat like this can transform a canine's mood in an instant. Sure enough, I immediately went from being an intruder to her new best friend. Feeling satisfied with being able to win her approval, I went to sleep off the day's intense activity.

> *The Pennsylvania Station in New York*
> *Is like some vast basilica of old*
> *That towers above the terrors of the dark*
> *As bulwark and protection to the soul.*
> *Now people who are hurrying alone*
> *And those who come in crowds from far away*
> *Pass through this great concourse of steel and stone*
> *To trains, or else from trains out into day.*

Langston Hughes

PEEKSKILL AND POUGHKIPSIE
SATURDAY - SEPTEMBER 22

The next morning witnessed a pleasant surprise. Doggie Dearest had opened the door of the room I was sleeping in to give me a lick on the cheek. This called for another piece of sausage and a dog biscuit. This was yet another verification of the saying that the way to a one's heart is often through the stomach. It applies equally to humans and canines. She gazed at me with such loving eyes, I forgot all about her temper tantrums the day before.

It was a pleasure to relax with my hosts and the pooches for a couple of hours. Out of several sites my cousin suggested that we could visit, I chose the Locust Manor, a mansion landscaped with beautiful gardens located just outside Poughkipsie on some bluffs overlooking the Hudson. It was an hour's drive north, so we set off right away.

The Manor lived up to its description. Once belonging to Samuel Morse, the inventor of the telegraph, a huge main house and adjacent carriage home were situated in the middle of a sprawling estate. They were surrounded by rows of colorful flowering pants and herbs. In front of the property was a gift shop and multi-purpose room where several people were planning a wedding reception to be held later that day. Behind the buildings were landscaped knolls that extended down to the river. It was a spectacular sight.

Too late for the last mansion tour, we strolled through grounds containing one of the loveliest collections of red, orange, yellow, pink, blue, and purple flowers I'd ever seen. Rows of dahlias, hollyhocks, cosmos, and other annuals overflowed with large blooms. Whoever tends this garden has ten green thumbs. Having picked a good time of year to visit this place, we were captivated by its amazing display,

After snapping photos, we walked behind the houses to the bluffs to view the Hudson. There, we met a female gardener. When we asked what we'd missed inside the mansion, she replied that the real beauty is outdoors. How fortunate she is to work in this environment. On our way out, we passed a large organic garden where the plants were so fertile they seemed to have been assisted by a magical force.

The drive back to Peekskill was slowed by commuter gridlock. Back home, we dined on Ukrainian restaurant leftovers, watched TV, played with the dogs, and called it a night.

PEEKSKILL TO PALM SPRINGS
SUNDAY - SEPTEMBER 23

Waking up on my last day of travel, my emotions were in conflict. Although I was eager to return home, I didn't want the journey to end. After a final tasty light breakfast with my cousin and her husband, I gave Doggie Dearest and her two companions some dog biscuits and played a round of fetch. Then I packed my things and she drove me to the train station for one last transit to Manhattan.

Like the previous day, I shared the car with a crowd of animated Yankee fans. I had trouble finding a seat when a young woman invited me over to one next to her.   I cheerfully accepted perhaps the last empty space on the coach. As we conversed, she shared that she was an educator who taught secondary school near Poughkipsie. Her work was getting more challenging each year. It was a struggle to keep the focus of students who weren't very motivated to learn. I told her that she was fortunate to have a job in that field because in my home state of California, teachers were being laid off in large numbers.

When we reached Yankee stadium, once again half the riders detrained. Shortly afterwards, I entered majestic Grand Central Station which was nowhere as crowded at this hour. Then I walked outside onto 42nd Avenue. I'd purposely arrived a couple of hours early so I could have a leisurely meal in the city before leaving for my flight home. Having only had a light snack, I was looking forward to a large breakfast. The Pershing Square Restaurant across the street looked appealing, especially with signs touting a Sunday brunch menu. I knew it might be expensive, but since this was my last fling on the road, I didn't mind.

I was seated at a table in a noisy room with ethnic servers in bow ties. I ordered a smoked salmon, spinach and goat cheese omelet that was served in terse, efficient, formal Manhattan style.   My Ukrainian waitress and Puerto Rican waiter were aloof and professional. Even the bus boys had a detached manor. This certainly wasn't LA, let alone my small high desert village. Though the price was double what I'd pay for the same thing in California, my meal was worth every dollar. The brusqueness of the service was refreshingly honest with no phony attempts to call me honey or sir or engage me in conversation. It was an uninterrupted and very memorable splurge.

Pershing Square Cafe, NY, NY

Back on the street, I wheeled my luggage to an airport shuttle depot my cousin had recommended. After a half hour wait, along with a dozen other travellers, I was led into a huge van blaring rap music. The fare was far less than a taxi. In any other city I might have been put off by the loud hip-hop, but it seemed to express a Manhattan vibe.   So I enjoyed it for the local color it provided.

At the airport, I had my first exposure to new security measures at the departure gates. I had to remove my shoes, take the toiletries out of my suitcase, and allow myself to be groped. I was tempted to tease the TSA agent "a little to the right" but I look a little Middle-Eastern in appearance and didn't want to tempt fate.

It was two hours before my flight, so I tried to relax in the noisy airport café. There I bought a $2 banana, the cheapest item at this tourist trap. It was chump change for a comfy wide seat at a table instead of the stiff narrow ones at the gates. My flight was delayed an extra hour, so I got my money's worth.

The flight to Denver was uneventful, except for the fact that not being in first class, I felt herded like cattle in a narrow coach seat, neither next to the window nor aisle. It seems to me that they've made the seats and legroom more compact in the past few years.

As we approached Denver, the jet encountered so much turbulence we couldn't land right away. The pilot announced that we'd be circling a few times around the airport until the winds died down. A woman sitting next to me said this was not unusual here because the airport is located right below the Rocky Mountains and subject to downdrafts. I wasn't especially thrilled to hear this. On the fourth approach, we finally were able to land.

Though I'd been dreading the two-hour wait between flights, we were over an hour behind schedule. I had to drag my luggage across the airport to my connecting flight to Palm Springs with little time to spare.   Hungry, I only had time to grab a quick meal to go for the next leg of my journey since only snacks were going to be served. I barely made it to the gate with fast food bag in hand.

Fortunately, this was a small commuter plane with a wide seat and a lot of room. By the time I finished my chicken salad sandwich and a complimentary airline soda, we were ready to make the long gradual descent over the California desert. I departed the gate in this relatively small airport to find myself in the kind of 100 degree midnight in Palm Springs heat that I'd forgotten all about. My friend was waiting to pick me up.   I was grateful to see him and to be safe at home once again.

We shall not cease from exploration
And the end of all our exploring
Will be to arrive where we started
And know the place for the first time.

T.S. Eliot

ABOUT THE AUTHOR

Cat Cohen was born in the 1940s near downtown LA and called the City Of Angels home for six decades before resettling in the high desert above Palm Springs. As a child he played along the walk of stars on Hollywood Boulevard and rubbed shoulders with the entertainment world early on, making two guest appearances on Art Linkletter's House Party TV show. At the age of ten his family moved to the Jewish neighborhood near Canter's Deli on Fairfax Avenue where he learned to fish pickles out of a barrel and haggle prices at local bakeries. His adolescence was spent in the San Fernando Valley before attending UCLA where he majored in music.

While enrolling in graduate school in classical composition, Cat also played in a rock band six nights a week in Redondo Beach. After a stint in the Peace Corps in Micronesia, he lived in Santa Monica a block from the ocean. Here he taught piano and wrote songs and musicals, several of which were recorded, produced, and performed. For many years he taught songwriting at UCLA Extension. During the 1980s he was involved in the political and social movements of LA's gay, HIV, and recovery communities, work he continues in the Coachella Valley today.

An active author member of the **Palm Springs Writers Guild**, Cat has nine self-published books on food, travel, and music including the international gourmet cookbook **Chicken Soups From Around The World**, the adventurous off-the-beaten-track **Road Stories Southwest** and **Road Poems, U.S.A.**, and his real estate memoir **My Desert Blog Cabin**. Cat's most recent book, his novel **The Longer Road Home**, is the story of Sam Freberg, a bohemian gay Jewish recovering addict who struggles through several decades of social liberation movements to find and heal himself in today's challenging world. www.catcohenauthor.com www.catcohen.com www.amazon.com/CatCohen/e/B00GG0QB74

[Photo by Joe Varga]